Guide To The Kindergarten

And Intermediate Class

By

Elizabeth Palmer Peabody

PREFACE.

CAMBRIDGE, Mass., March 1, 1869.

SINCE publishing the first edition of what I meant to be a Guide to those who undertake to give Kindergarten culture, I have been in Europe, and made a special study of the Kindergartens established in Hamburgh, Berlin, and Dresden, by Froebel himself, and his most distinguished scholars.

This study has more and more confirmed the conviction I derived from reading Froebel's "Essay on the Education of the Human Race;" viz., that no greater benefit could be conferred on our country, than the far and wide spread of Kindergartens, *as an underpinning,* so to say, of our noble public-school system, giving adequate moral foundation, thoroughness, and practicality to the national education.

But I also learned that no book could be written that would make an expert Kindergartner. It was the careful observations and earnest experiments of half a century, that gave to Froebel himself that profound knowledge of childhood which enabled him to formulate the principles, deduce the rules, and call forth the spirit of a genuine art of education. But though no genius and industry less than his own could have originated this art, any soundly cultured, intelligent, genial-tempered young woman, who loves children, can appreciate and practise it, if—and only if—she is trained by a living teacher engaged in the work at the moment.

This, I myself have proved experimentally also; for *my* knowledge was first obtained only from books. I had the best manuals and guides, but did not know that they were intended merely for the convenience of already trained teachers; and that they necessarily omitted the characteristic peculiarity of the method, because *written words* cannot do justice to the fine steps by which the child is led to gradually carry its total spontaneity forwards, on every plane of its little life,—artistic, moral, and intellectual.

For there is nothing merely mechanical and imitative in true Kindergarten culture: the child acts "from within outwards" in every thing it does, however seemingly trifling; and, if we use the word *artist* in its most general sense, becomes an artist from the beginning. Thus is prevented that too common divorce between the powers of thinking and acting, whose harmony ensures ability in a strict proportion to intellectual capacity. Consciousness of aim, and enjoyment of success, at every step develop new ideas and power, and fulfil that law of nature by which thought tends to rush into act instantly, as in childish play. Nothing is more melancholy in experience than to see people *drifting* instead of *living*; but this general failure of human life is owing to the fact, that the unassisted child is baffled in its will and balked of its desires, by a want of that steadiness of aim, perseverance, and knowledge of how to adapt means to ends, which adult sympathy and wisdom should supply; and from want of which it loses the original harmony of its being in the process of its growth. Kindergarten culture is the adult mind entering into the child's world, and appreciating nature's intention as displayed in every impulse of spontaneous life; and so directing it that the joy of success may be ensured at every step, and artistic things be actually produced, which gives the self-reliance and conscious intelligence that ought to discriminate human power from blind force.

The only mistake in idea which I see that I made in my "Guide," was making it the object of the teacher to cultivate the *individualities* of each pupil especially. This is not even desirable, and would require the intuitive genius of Froebel in every single teacher. In a true art of education, individualities will be tenderly respected; but it is not what is individual, but what is common to all (or that universal of human nature which rises into the divine creative), which is to be cultivated especially. Every process of Froebel's Kindergarten is good for all children, and, interfering with nothing original, leaves their individualities free to express themselves *sufficiently*. For individual varieties are irrefragable, and give piquancy and beauty to human life, except they are pampered,—when they become deformities. To follow universal laws in their orderly development, ensures a necessary harmony with others, while a margin is always to be left for *invention*, which is what gives conscious freedom, and makes obedience no longer blind and passive, but intelligent and active; every healthy instinct and affection becoming at last spiritual law.

Nevertheless, I gladly meet the demand of the public for a second edition of the "Guide," because its defect is not in its spirit and general idea, seeing that it has awakened an interest in Kindergartens all over the United States, as numerous letters from all parts have proved to me; but in my having somewhat confused what belongs to the second and third stages of primary education, with a preliminary process, which it is necessary not only to begin with, but to keep distinct for a considerable time, until the habit of mind is formed of asking clearly what is going to be done before attempting to do it. What I missed cannot be supplied by any book; for this preliminary process can only be learned from the living teaching of the Normal class. I make some revisory notes, also change some thirty pages, and gladly embrace the opportunity, which the popularity of my "Guide" gives me, to make known, as far as it goes abroad, that, when I came home from Europe, I found what I had seen to be the indispensable condition of an effective introduction of Froebel's art into either the private or public education of America; viz., a training-school for Kindergartners, actually established by Madame Kriege in Boston (127 Charles Street), in connection with a Kindergarten to be taught by her daughter, fresh from the school of Berlin, founded by the Baroness Marienholtz, a noble lady who has devoted her pen, her fortune, the prestige of her rank, and even her personal services, to the diffusion of Kindergarten culture on the continent of Europe.

The so-called Kindergarten which I had established, was gladly given up to make room for this genuine one; and I have the highest expectations from the Normal training. Already several teachers, who had made experiments of their own, which had taught them the need of this special instruction, have engaged themselves as Madame Kriege's pupils; and the spread of the demand for Kindergartners will, I think, keep her Normal class always full. I cannot but hope that the time may come when the Normal schools of all our States may be endowed with a professorship of Kindergarten culture adequately filled.

Omitting my own preface to my first edition, I retain as explanation of the origin of the letters on moral culture, which make the last part of the "Guide," and give it its greatest value to mothers, Mrs. Mann's

POSTSCRIPT.

CONTENTS.

CHAP.		PAGE
I.	Kindergarten—What Is It?	9
II.	Rooms, Etc.	19
III.	Music	22
IV.	Plays, Gymnastics, and Dancing	28
V.	The Kindergartner	35
VI.	Kindergarten Occupations	43
VII.	Moral and Religious Exercises	54
VIII.	Object Lessons	58
IX.	Geometry	65
X.	Reading	71
XI.	Grammar and Languages	98
XII.	Geography	103
XIII.	The Secret of Power	104

CHAPTER I.

KINDERGARTEN—WHAT IS IT?

WHAT is a Kindergarten? I will reply by negatives. It is not the old-fashioned infant-school. That was a narrow institution, comparatively; the object being (I do not speak of Pestalozzi's own, but that which we have had in this country and in England) to take the children of poor laborers, and keep them out of the fire and the streets, while their mothers went to their necessary labor. Very good things, indeed, in their way. Their principle of discipline was to circumvent the wills of children, in every way that would enable their teachers to keep them within bounds, and quiet. It was certainly better that they should learn to sing *by rote* the Creed and the "definitions" of scientific terms, and such like, than to learn the profanity and obscenity of the streets, which was the alternative. But no mother who wished for anything which might be called the *development* of her child would think of putting it into an infant-school, especially if she lived in the country, amid

> "the mighty sum
> Of things forever speaking,"

where any "old grey stone" would altogether surpass, as a stand-point, the bench of the highest class of an infant-school. In short, they did not state the problem of infant culture with any breadth, and accomplished nothing of general interest on the subject.

Neither is the primary public school a Kindergarten, though it is but justice to the capabilities of that praiseworthy institution, so important in default of a better, to say that in one of them, at the North End of Boston, an enterprising and genial teacher has introduced one feature of Froebel's plan. She has actually given to each of her little children a box of playthings, wherewith to amuse itself according to its own sweet will, at all times when not under direct instruction,—necessarily, in her case, on condition of its being perfectly quiet; and this one thing makes this primary school the best one in Boston, both as respects the attainments of the scholars and their good behavior.

Kindergarten means a garden of children, and Froebel, the inventor of it, or rather, as he would prefer to express it, *the discoverer of the method of Nature,* meant to symbolize by the name the spirit and plan of treatment. How does the gardener treat his plants? He studies their individual natures, and puts them into such circumstances of soil and atmosphere as enable them to grow, flower, and bring forth fruit,—also to renew their manifestation year after year. He does not expect to succeed unless he learns all their wants, and the circumstances in which these wants will be supplied, and all their possibilities of beauty and use, and the means of giving them opportunity to be perfected. On the other hand, while he knows that they must not be forced against their individual natures, he does not leave them to grow wild, but prunes redundancies, removes destructive worms and bugs from their leaves and stems, and weeds from their vicinity, —carefully watching to learn what peculiar insects affect what particular plants, and how the former can be destroyed without injuring the vitality of the latter. After all the most careful gardener can do, he knows that the form of the plant is predetermined in the germ or seed, and that the inward tendency must concur with a multitude of influences, the most powerful and subtile of which is removed in place ninety-five millions of miles away.

In the Kindergarten, *children* are treated on an analogous plan. It presupposes gardeners of the mind, who are quite aware that they have as little power to override the characteristic individuality of a child, or to predetermine this characteristic, as the gardener of plants to say that a lily shall be a rose. But notwithstanding this limitation on one side, and the necessity for a concurrence of the Spirit on the other,—which is more independent of our modification than the remote sun,—yet they must feel responsible, after all, for the perfection of the development, in so far as removing every impediment, preserving every condition, and pruning every redundance.

This analogy of education to the gardener's art is so striking, both as regards what we can and what we cannot do, that Froebel has put every educator into a most suggestive Normal School, by the very word which he has given to his seminary,—Kindergarten.

If every school-teacher in the land had a garden of flowers and fruits to cultivate, it could hardly fail that he would learn to be wise in his vocation. For suitable preparation, the first, second, and third thing is, to

> "Come forth into the light of things,
> Let Nature be your teacher."

The "new education," as the French call it, begins with children in the mother's arms. Froebel had the nurses bring to his establishment, in Hamburg, children who could not talk, who were not more than three months old, and trained the nurses to work on his principles and by his methods. This will hardly be done in this country, at least at present; but to supply the place of such a class, a lady of Boston has prepared and published, under copyright, Froebel's First Gift, consisting of six soft balls of the three primary and the three secondary colors, which are sold in a box, with a little manual for mothers, in which the true principle and plan of tending babies, so as not to rasp their nerves, but to amuse without wearying them, is very happily suggested. There is no mother or nurse who would not be assisted by this little manual essentially. As it says in the beginning,—"Tending babies is an art, and every art is founded on a science of observations; for love is not wisdom, but love must act *according to wisdom* in order to succeed. Mothers and nurses, however tender and kind-hearted, may, and oftenest do, weary and vex the nerves of children, in well-meant efforts to amuse them, and weary themselves the while. Froebel's exercises, founded on the observations of an intelligent sensibility, are intended to amuse without wearying, to educate without vexing."

Froebel's Second Gift for children, adapted to the age from one to two or three years, with another little book of directions, has also been published by the same lady, and is perhaps a still greater boon to every nursery; for this is the age when many a child's temper is ruined, and the inclination of the twig wrongly bent, through sheer *want of resource and idea*, on the part of nurses and mothers.

But it is to the next age—from three years old and upwards—that the Kindergarten becomes the desideratum, if not a necessity. The isolated home, made into a flower-vase by the application of the principles set forth in the Gifts above mentioned, may do for babies. But every mother and nurse knows how hard it is to meet the demands of a child too young to be taught to read, but whose opening intelligence and irrepressible bodily activity are so hard to be met by an adult, however genial and active. Children generally take the temper of their whole lives from this period of their existence. Then "the twig is bent," either towards that habit of self-defence which is an ever-renewing cause of selfishness, or to the sun of love-in-exercise, which is the exhaustless source of goodness and beauty.[A]

The indispensable thing now is a sufficient society of children. It is only in the society of equals that the social instinct can be gratified, and come into equilibrium with the instinct of self-preservation. Self-love, and love of others, are equally natural; and before reason is developed, and the proper spiritual life begins, sweet and beautiful childhood may bloom out and imparadise our mortal life. Let us only give the social instinct of children its fair chance. For this purpose, a few will not do. The children of one family are not enough, and do not come along fast enough. A large company should be gathered out of many families. It will be found that the little things are at once taken out of themselves, and become interested in each other. In the variety, affinities develop themselves very prettily, and the rough points of rampant individualities wear off. We have seen a highly-gifted child, who, at home, was—to use a vulgar, but expressive word—pesky and odious, with the exacting demands of a powerful, but untrained mind and heart, become "sweet as roses" spontaneously, amidst the rebound of a large, well-ordered, and carefully watched child-society. Anxious mothers have brought us children, with a thousand deprecations and explanations of their characters, as if they thought we were going to find them little monsters, which their motherly hearts were persuaded they were not, though they behaved like little sanchos at home,—and, behold, they were as harmonious, from the very beginning, as if they had undergone the subduing influence of a lifetime. We are quite sure that children begin with loving others quite as intensely as they love themselves,—forgetting themselves in their love of others,—if they only have as fair a chance of being benevolent and self-sacrificing as of being selfish. Sympathy is as much a natural instinct as self-love, and no more or less innocent, in a moral point of view. Either principle alone makes an ugly and depraved form of natural character. Balanced, they give the element of happiness, and the conditions of spiritual goodness and truth,—making children fit temples for the Holy Ghost to dwell in.

A Kindergarten, then, is children in society,—a commonwealth or republic of children,—whose laws are all part and parcel of the Higher Law alone. It may be contrasted, in every particular, with the old-fashioned school, which is an absolute monarchy, where the children are subjected to a lower expediency, having for its prime end quietness, or such order as has "reigned in Warsaw" since 1831.

But let us not be misunderstood. We are not of those who think that children, in any condition whatever, will inevitably develop into beauty and goodness. Human nature tends to revolve in a vicious circle, around the idiosyncrasy; and children must have over them, in the person of a wise and careful teacher, a power which shall deal with them as God deals with the mature, presenting the claims of sympathy and truth whenever they presumptuously or unconsciously fall into selfishness. We have the best conditions of moral culture in a company large enough for the exacting disposition of the solitary child to be balanced by the claims made by others on the common stock of enjoyment,—there being a reasonable oversight of older persons, wide-awake to anticipate, prevent, and adjust the rival pretensions which must always arise where there are finite beings with infinite desires, while Reason, whose proper object is God, is yet undeveloped.

Let the teacher always take for granted that the law of love is quick within, whatever are appearances, and the better self will generally respond. In proportion as the child is young and unsophisticated, will be the certainty of the response to a teacher of simple faith:

> "There are who ask not if thine eye
>   Be on them,—who, in love and truth,
> Where no misgiving is, rely
>   Upon the genial sense of youth.
>
> "And blest are they who in the main
> This faith even now do entertain,

> Live in the spirit of this creed,
> Yet find another strength, according to their need."

That "other strength" is to be found in recognition of the Eternal laws of order, and reverent application of them to human action. But children must receive this from the Kindergartner, who shall give them such help in embodying their ever-springing fancies as shall prevent "the weight of chance desires," and issue in a tangible success, by entering into and carrying forward their total, spontaneous activity, without destroying its childishness.

One of the most important exercises for children in the Kindergarten is block building. A box of eight little cubes is so managed that it will unfold in the child's mind the law of symmetry, by means of series of forms which the children are led to make in a way rather difficult to describe here. So quick are the fancies of children, that the blocks will serve also as symbols of every thing in Nature and imagination. We have seen an ingenious teacher assemble a class of children around her large table, to each of whom she had given the blocks. The first thing was to count them, a great process of arithmetic to most of them. Then she made something and explained it. It was perhaps a light-house,—and some blocks would represent rocks near it to be avoided, and ships sailing in the ocean; or perhaps it was a hen-coop, with chickens inside, and a fox prowling about outside, and a boy who was going to catch the fox and save the fowls. Then she told each child to make something, and when it was done hold up a hand. The first one she asked to explain, and then went round the class. If one began to speak before another had ended, she would hold up her finger and say,—"It is not your turn." In the course of the winter, she taught, over these blocks, a great deal about the habits of animals. She studied natural history in order to be perfectly accurate in her symbolic representation of the habitation of each animal, and their enemies were also represented by blocks. The children imitated these; and when they drew upon their imaginations for facts, and made fantastic creations, she would say,—"Those, I think, were fairy hens" (or whatever); for it was her principle to accept everything, and thus tempt out their invention. The great value of this exercise is to get them into the habit of representing something they have thought by an outward symbol. The explanations they are always eager to give, teach them to express themselves in words. Full scope is given to invention, whether in the direction of possibilities or of the impossibilities in which children's imaginations revel,—in either case the child being trained to the habit of embodiment of its thought.

Froebel thought it very desirable to have a garden where the children could cultivate flowers. He had one which he divided into lots for the several children, reserving a portion for his own share in which they could assist him. He thought it the happiest mode of calling their attention to the invisible God, whose power must be waited upon, after the conditions for growth are carefully arranged according to *laws* which they must observe. Where a garden is impossible, a flower-pot with a plant in it, for each child to take care of, would do very well.

But the best way to cultivate a sense of the presence of God is to draw the attention to the conscience, which is very active in children, and which seems to them (as we all can testify from our own remembrance) another than themselves, and yet themselves. We have heard a person say, that in her childhood she was puzzled to know which was herself, the voice of her inclination or of her conscience, for they were palpably two; and what a joyous thing it was when she was first convinced that one was the Spirit of God, whom unlucky teaching had previously embodied in a form of terror on a distant judgment-seat. Children are consecrated as soon as they get the spiritual idea, and it may be so presented that it shall make them happy as well as true. But the adult who enters into such conversation with a child must be careful not to shock and profane, instead of nurturing the soul. It is possible to avoid both discouraging and flattering views, and to give the most tender and elevating associations.

But children require not only an alternation of physical and mental amusements, but some instruction to be passively received. They delight in stories, and a wise teacher can make this subservient to the highest uses by reading beautiful creations of the imagination. Not only such household-stories as "Sanford and Merton," Mrs. Farrar's "Robinson Crusoe," and Salzmann's "Elements of Morality," but symbolization like the heroes of Asgard, the legends of the Middle Ages, classic and chivalric tales, the legend of Saint George, and "Pilgrim's Progress," can in the mouth of a skilful reader be made subservient to moral culture. The reading sessions should not exceed ten or fifteen minutes.

Anything of the nature of scientific teaching should be done by presenting *objects* for examination and investigation.[B] Flowers and insects, shells, etc., are easily handled. The observations should be drawn out of the children, not made to them, except as corrections of their mistakes. Experiments with the prism, and in crystallization and transformation, are useful and desirable to awaken taste for the sciences of Nature. In short, the Kindergarten should give the beginnings of everything. "What is well begun is half done."

We must say a word about the locality and circumstances of a Kindergarten. There is published in Lausanne, France, a newspaper devoted to the interests of this mode of education, in whose early numbers is described a Kindergarten which seems to be of the nature of a boarding-school; at least, the children are there all day. Each child has a garden, and there is one besides where they work in common. There are accommodations for keeping animals, and miniature tools to do mechanical labor of various kinds. In short, it is a child's world. But in this country, especially in New England, parents would not consent to be so much separated from their children, and a few hours of Kindergarten in the early part of the day will serve an excellent purpose,—using up the effervescent activity of children, who may healthily be left to themselves the rest of the time, to play or rest, comparatively unwatched.

Two rooms are indispensable, if there is any variety of age. It is desirable that one should be sequestrated to the quiet employments. A pianoforte is desirable, to lead the singing, and accompany the plays, gymnastics, frequent marchings, and dancing, when that is taught,—which it should be. But a hand-organ which plays fourteen tunes will help to supply the want of a piano, and a guitar in the hands of a ready teacher will do better than nothing.

Sometimes a genial mother and daughters might have a Kindergarten, and devote themselves and the house to it, especially if they live in one of our beautiful country-towns or cities. The habit, in the city of New York, of sending children to school in an omnibus, hired to go round the city and pick them up, suggests the possibility of a Kindergarten in one of those beautiful residences up in town, where there is a garden before or behind the house. It is impossible to keep Kindergarten *by the way*. It must be the main business of those who undertake it; for it is necessary that every individual child should be borne, as it were, on the heart of the *gardeners*, in order that it be *inspired* with order, truth, and goodness. To develop a child from within outwards, we must plunge ourselves into its peculiarity of imagination and feeling. No one person could possibly endure such absorption of life in labor unrelieved, and consequently two or three should unite in the undertaking in order to be able to relieve each other from the enormous strain on life. The compensations are, however, great. The charm of the various individuality, and of the refreshing presence of conscience yet unprofaned, is greater than can be found elsewhere in this work-day world. Those were not idle words which came from the lips of Wisdom Incarnate: —"Their angels do always behold the face of my Father:" "Of such is the kingdom of heaven."

CHAPTER II.

ROOMS, ETC.

I HAVE made an article, which I published in the "Atlantic Monthly" of November, 1862, my first chapter, because I cannot, in any better way, answer the general question,—What is a Kindergarten? I will now proceed to make a Guide for the conduct of a Kindergarten; in which I shall freely make use of what Madame Rongé has said in her "English Kindergarten," and Madame Marienholtz in her "Jardin des Enfans;" but I shall not confine myself to them, for an American Kindergarten necessarily has its peculiarities.

In the first place, we must think of the accommodations. These are not to be in the open air, as has been supposed by many, through misapprehension of the use of the word Kindergarten. But it is desirable that there should be a good play-ground attached to the rooms; and Froebel thought it of very important religious influence that every child should have earth to cultivate, if it were only a foot square.

Two rooms are indispensable, and if possible there should be three, all of good size, with good light and air: one room for music and plays, gymnastics, dancing, &c.; another for the quieter mechanical employments, —pricking, weaving, sewing, moulding, folding, paper-cutting, sticklaying, and block-building; and still another for drawing, writing, object-teaching, and learning to read. It is desirable that every child should have a box, if not a little desk, in order to learn to keep things in order. When this cannot be done, the teachers must so arrange matters, as to have everything ready for every change; that no time may be lost and no confusion arise. In my own Kindergarten, I arrange beforehand the chairs in the play-room in a solid square, into which the children march at the commencement of the exercises. Sitting in them, they sing their morning prayer or hymn, hear the reading, and take a singing lesson on the scale. Then they rise, and, taking up their chairs, march into the other room for their reading lessons, which are always in two classes, sometimes in three. They bring their chairs back again for luncheon, and then take them out for another lesson; for in this room they have gymnastics, dancing, and the play, and need a clear space for all. They come back with their chairs, at the close of the exercises, to sing songs together before they disperse. Two of my rooms are carpeted. The other is smooth-floored for dancing, playing, and gymnastics. And, for the convenience of the gymnastics, it is well to paint, at convenient distances, *little feet in the first position*, as Dr. Dio Lewis has done in his gymnastic hall.

When Kindergarten accommodations can be built expressly, I would suggest that there should be a house with glass walls and partitions, at least above the wainscoting; and that the wainscoting should be rather high and painted black, so that every child might have a piece of the blackboard; for it is easier for a child to draw with a chalk on a blackboard than with a slate and pencil.

A house of glass, on the plan of the crystal palace, would be no more expensive than if built of brick. It would secure the light and sunshine, and make it easy for the superintendent to overlook the whole. It should be equably warmed throughout. My own Kindergarten is not in a glass house, but is the lower floor of a house which has three rooms, with a hall between two of the rooms; a large china closet which I use for the children's dressing, as well as to store many things; and beyond the third room, a bathing room, with every convenience. Rooms, hall, closet, and bathing room have all an east-south aspect, and are amply lighted. The room between the china closet and bathing room is longer than it is wide, and has blackboard painted on three sides of it, so that each child has a piece of blackboard.

It is possible to keep a Kindergarten in two rooms, but not possible to keep it in one, if it is of any desirable size, or there is any variety of age in the children. A large play-ground and some garden is desirable. I am so fortunate as to have these in my house in Boston.

The tables for the children to sit at should be low; and it is a good plan to have them painted in squares of an inch; chequered, or ruled by lines, so that they may be able always to set their blocks down with perfect accuracy.

One of the rooms it would be well to provide with *flat* box-desks, in which can be kept all the materials which each child uses,—slates and pencils, blocks, sticks, weaving and sewing materials,—and the children should be required to keep these in order.

In my own Kindergarten I provide all the materials for their work and instruction, thus securing uniformity; and it is better to do so always, and to charge a price covering the expense. It should be understood, from the first, that Kindergarten education is not cheap.

As a Kindergarten requires several persons to keep it properly, a genial family, consisting of a mother and daughters, of various accomplishments, might devote their whole house to it, preparing for the writing and drawing one large room with blackboards all round, whose area could be used for the playing, gymnastics, and dancing.

When this new culture shall be appreciated for its whole worth, it will not be deemed extravagant for a whole family thus to devote their house, as well as their time, to make a Kindergarten the temporary home of a large company of children.

CHAPTER III.

MUSIC.

The first requisite to the Kindergarten is Music. The voice of melody commands the will of the child, or rather disarms the caprice, which is the principle of disorder. Two hymns are given in this Guide with which to commence school,—one being the Lord's Prayer, set to cheerful music.

But there should be regular scale singing, and if conducted by a teacher of tact, a ten minutes lesson may be given every day, and the interest be kept undiminished. The first lesson should be preceded by the teacher's drawing on the blackboard a ladder of eight steps, and then saying to the pupils, "Now listen to my voice, and see how it goes up these steps." She then sings the eight notes very clearly, pointing to each step of the ladder; and runs her voice, with equal distinctness, down the descending scale. The children can then be asked to accompany the teacher in going up and down the ladder, singing the numbers 1, 2, 3, 4, 5, 6, 7, 8, instead of *do, re, mi*. There will doubtless be enough discords to be palpable to all ears, and these can be spoken of by the teacher, and a proposition made that every one who thinks he can go up and down the ladder alone, shall hold up a hand. Some may be able to do so, but a majority will fail. Some will not try at all.

The teacher can then say, "Now I am going to teach you all to do it,—one step at a time. Let us all sing *one*." The piano is struck, and teacher and pupils all sing *one*. "Now let us go up a step,—one, two." Let this be repeated several times. Then stop, and say, "Now I am going to strike one of these notes and see if you know it." Strike two, and ask, "What is that, 1 or 2?" There may be difference of opinion; in which case, ask all to "hold up their hands who think it is 2, and then all who think it is 1." Tell which is right, and say, "Now let us all sing 2." Then say, "Now let us go down that step,—2, 1; and now up again,—1, 2; now all hold up their hands who can sing 1, 2, 1?" Select one after another to sing it alone with the piano, and after each has tried, let all sing with the teacher 1, 2, 1, before another is asked to sing it. Then let all sing 1, 1, 1; 2, 2, 2; 1, 1, 1. Go on in this way till all the eight notes are learned. They will be able to tell these notes, when struck upon the piano, much sooner than they will be able to strike them with their voices. And other exercises, every day calling upon them to name notes struck,—at first one note, afterwards combinations of notes.

The following exercises were given in my Kindergarten in one year, which resulted in nearly all the children being able to sing them alone, and tell any notes struck.

1st.—1 2 1; 1 1, 2 2, 1 1; 1 1 1 1, 2 2 2 2, 1 1 1 1 2 1 2, &c.

2d.—1 2 3, 3 2 1; 1 3 3 1, 1 2 1, 2 3 2, 3 2 1.

3d.—1 2 3 4 5, 5 4 3 2 1. 1 3 5, 5 3 1, 1 5 5 1.

4th.—1 2 3 4 5 6; 6 5 4 3 2 1; 1 6, 6 1; 1 3 5 6.

5th.—1 2 3 4 5 6 7, 7 6 5 4 3 2 1; 1 3 5 8, 8 5 3 1.

6th.—1 2 3 4 5 6 7 8, 8 7 5 6 4 3 2 1; 1 3 5 8.

This exercise can be varied by repeating each note one two, three, or four times.

7th.—1 1 2, 2 2 3, 3 3 4, 4 4 5, 5 5 6, 7 7 8, 8 7 6 5 4 3 2 1.

8th.—1 1 2, 3 3 4, 5 5 6, 7 7 8; 8 7 6 5 4 3 2 1.

9th.—1 2, 1 2 1; 2 3, 2 3 2; 3 4, 3 4 3; 4 5, 4 5 6; 5 6, 5 6 7; 6 7, 6 7 8; 8, 7, 6, 5, 4, 3, 2, 1.

10th.—1 1, 2 2, 1; 2 2, 3 3, 2; 3 3, 4 4, 3; 4 4, 5 5, 4; &c.

11th.—1 3; 2 4; 3 5; 4 6; 5 7; 6 8; 8, 6; 7, 5; 6, 4; 5, 3; 4, 2; 3, 1.

12th.—1 3 5 8, 8 5 3 1; 1 4 6 8, 8 6 4 1; 1 8 8 1.

13th.—1 1, 3 3; 5 5, 8 8; 8 8, 7 7, 6 6, 5 5, 4 4, 3 3, 2 2, 1 1.

14th.—1 2 3 2 1; 2 3 4 3 2; 3 4 5 4 3; 4 5 6 5 4; 5 6 7 6 5; 6 7 8 7 6; 7 8 7 6 5 4 3 2 1.

15th.—1 2 1 2 3 3; 2 3 2 3 4 4; 3 4 3 4 5 5; 4 5 4 5 6 6; 5 6 5 6 7 7; 6 7 6 7 8 8; 8 8 8 8; 7 7 7 7; 6 6 6 6; 5 5 5 5; 4 4 4 4; 3 3 3 3; 2 2 2 2; 1 1 1 1; 1 8; 8 1.

Besides these ten minutes on the scale, (which should not occur next to singing the hymn, but after some other exercise has intervened,) it is an excellent plan to let the Kindergarten close with singing songs by rote. The words should be simple, such as "The Cat and the Sparrow," and other pretty melodies to be found in the Pestalozzian Singing Book and the many compilations prepared for children. For it is well for the child not to go out of the natural octave, and to have the words of songs adapted to the childish capacity. Besides this singing, the piano-forte should be used to play marches, as the children go from one room to another to their different exercises. "Order is Heaven's first law," and music is the heavenly voice of order, which disposes to gentleness and regularity of motion. As all the exercises change every quarter of an hour at least, this brings the marching to music as often; and it will last one or two minutes, sometimes longer. The children get accustomed to rise at the sound of the piano, and it will be easy to make them silent during the music, especially if it is hinted to them that *soldiers* always march in silence. Besides this, the piano is necessary for the gymnastics, and for the fanciful plays, which are always to be accompanied by descriptive songs.

A few songs and plays are given in this Guide which, if taken in turn, will recur not oftener than once in ten days. We subjoin a description of the plays.

I will finish this chapter by a translation from a notice of "Enseignement Musical, d'aprés Froebel, par Fred. Stern, prix, 2 francs: En vente à Bruxelles, rue de Vienne, 16, et à Paris, rue Fossés St. Victor, 35." "A man to be complete, should be master of linear and musical expression. Most of our education aims only to give him lingual expression; and drawing and music are considered accomplishments merely! The divine art which enables us to reproduce the human figure illuminated with the expression of the spirit, a mere accomplishment![C] Music, the melodious expression of our most intimate thoughts, the colored reflection of the heart,—a mere accomplishment!

"Life is sad, monotonous, earthy, without the arts. If a woman of the middle and higher classes especially, does not daily realize the higher life by knowledge of truth and love of beauty, what shall save her from the frivolity and *ennui* that gnaws away the heart, tarnishes the soul, and brings misfortune to the fireside? Every woman should be an artist, and make artists of her children, if she would do a woman's whole duty. Especially should the mother teach her children to *improvise* music, which can be done by pursuing this method.

"He commences by the study of the three sounds constituting the major triad, and, as in the model gamut, *or gamut of do*, there are three similar triads, three perfect major chords, do-mi-sol, fa-la-do, and sol-si-re, we begin naturally with the central chord, do-mi-sol, which we name the master chord; for, in the model gamut of do, it is around this, as around a centre, that the two other triads balance themselves, the lower fifth, fa-la-do, and the higher fifth, sol-si-re. We can show the unity of plan between these three established notes, in all the possible changes. We thus introduce a fine variety into the exercises, which permits the repetition of the same sounds and intervals, without causing fatigue or weariness to the child.

"Scarcely have our pupils learned to sing or to repeat alone, at will, the three sounds do-mi-sol, when we have them mark them with pencils on the staff (key of sol); only as in the unity of tone there are yet the two other perfect chords, fa-la-do and sol-si-re, we let them write the three notes of the central chord with a red pencil, and reserve the three sounds of the chord on the left, (the lower or subdominant,) to be written with a yellow pencil, and the chord on the right, (higher or dominant,) with a blue pencil. On the other hand, for the appellative chords (dissonant,) made by the combination of the chord sol-si-re, with one, two, and even three notes of the chord fa-la-do, we use green pencils (mixture of blue and yellow). For we would keep the theory in mind by visible signs, which act most powerfully upon the minds of children.

"Then we pass to perfect minor chords, and terminate this first branch of our method by the study of the gamut.

"Our pupil knows as yet only a single tone,—the tone of *do*, which we designate by the name of model tone;—but all musicians are aware that to know well one tone, is to know them all, since they are all calculated on the model tone with which we began. The second part of our method will treat of the other tones, but it will prove no serious difficulty to our pupil.

"We have carefully avoided scientific terms, though doubtless, by a learned terminology, we should have struck superficial minds more. But we address ourselves to the serious, who know that it is better to know a thing in itself, (in what constitutes it essentially,) without knowing its technology, than to know obscure terms and be ignorant of the thing.

"Later, we shall initiate our pupil into the language generally adopted by all treatises on harmony. We wish that one day he may be a distinguished harmonist, knowing musical grammar at the foundation. It is strange that the study of grammar, so vigorously recommended for all other languages, is so entirely neglected in respect to musical language. The study of harmony seems to be reserved exclusively to artists; and even among them, only the few who are occupied with composing devote themselves to it with any profoundness. It is to this culpable negligence that we must attribute the difficulties of musical education. Where is the intelligent musician who would dare to deny the happy results inseparable from the most profound study of music? The scholar would necessarily have to give much less time to know the art in the best manner, which is now accessible only to remarkable persons of strong will. The grammatical study of music should begin at the same time as all other studies, and soon music would become the language of all, instead of being reserved exclusively to the privileged.

"Doubtless great reforms will be necessary to arrive at this result, and the spirit of routine which unhappily reigns everywhere will render such reforms difficult.

"However, we found great hopes on the inevitable development of the method of Froebel, for the principles he lays down are of general application."...

I am myself so profoundly impressed with the importance of little children's beginning music in this manner, that, having found a teacher who is capable of it, I intend, another year, to have extra hours for those who will commence instrumental music, in my own Kindergarten; so that each child can have a lesson *every day,* and only play under the eye of the teacher until quite expert.

CHAPTER IV.

PLAYS, GYMNASTICS, AND DANCING.

In playing <u>The Pigeon-house</u>, the teacher, who should always play with the children, takes three quarters of the number, and forms them into a circle, while the other quarter remains in the middle, to represent the pigeons.

The circle is the pigeon-house, and sings the song, beginning with the words:

"We open the pigeon-house again,"

while, standing still, they all hold up their joined hands, so as to let all the pigeons out at the word "open;" and, as the circle goes round singing,

"And let all the happy flutterers free,
They fly o'er the fields and grassy plain.
Delighted with glorious liberty,"

the pigeons run round, waving their hands up and down to imitate flying. At the word "return," in the line

"And when they return from their joyous flight,"

the joined hands of those in circle are lifted up again, and the pigeons go in. Then the pigeon-house closes round them, bowing their heads, and singing,

"We shut up the house and bid them good-night,"

which is repeated while the circle swings off and again comes together bowing.

The play can be done over until all in turn have been pigeons.

In playing <u>Hare in the Hollow</u>, a fourth of the children sit in the middle, on their hands and feet, while the rest, in circle, go round singing the three verses, and when the words "jump and spring," in the last verse, occur, the circle stops, and the joined hands are lifted up, and all the children leap out and around, on their hands and feet, (not knees,)—while the last lines are repeated twice.

In THE CUCKOOS, a circle is formed, or two concentric circles, and four children are put in the four corners of the room to enact cuckoos. The cuckoos sing "cuckoo," and those children in the circle answer; and when the words of the song indicate that the cuckoos should join the children, all four burst into the circle, and those who are found at their right hands become cuckoos the next time.

Almost like this last is the play of THE BEES; one child being put in the corner as a drone, and at the word "*Beware*," the drone breaks into the circle.

THE WINDMILL is done by dividing the children into companies of four, and letting them cross right hands and go round, and then cross left hands and go round the opposite way. By a change of the word *windmill* to *water-wheel*, the same music will serve for another play, in which there is a large circle formed, and then four or six spokes are made by six crossing hands in the middle, and then one or more children lengthening each spoke, and joining it to the circle, which forms the rim of the wheel. This is a more romping play than either of the foregoing, as the different velocities of those who are at the centre and circumference make it nearly impossible to have the motions correspond in time; but it is great fun, and serves for a change.

THE CLAPPERS IN THE CORN-MILL is made by one or by two concentric circles, going round as they sing the words; and the beauty of it consists in their minding the pauses and clapping in time. Whenever there are concentric circles, as is often necessary, when there are many children, the circles should move in different directions, and all circular motions must be frequently reversed.

In THE SAWYERS, the children stand facing each other in couples, in a circle, and move their joined hands from shoulder to shoulder in time to the music of the first verse. In singing the second verse, they skip round with their partners.

In THE WHEEL-BARROW, they are also arranged in couples, back to front; the front child leaning over to imitate the barrow, and stretching his hands behind him, which the child at his back takes as if to wheel. When the words are repeated the children reverse.

In THE COOPERS, the children, who form the barrels or hogshead, stand back to front in a circle, each taking hold of the waist of the one before him. The coopers walk round outside in time, at every third step pounding on the shoulder of the child nearest him in the barrel. When the word "around" comes, the barrel must begin to turn, and the coopers stand still, pounding on the shoulders of each child as he passes.

In THE LITTLE MASTER OF GYMNASTICS, each child in turn stands in the middle of the circle, and makes any motion he chooses, which all the rest imitate.

EQUAL TREADING is done in a circle, or in two concentric circles.

In WE LIKE TO GO A-ROVING, the children march round freely within sound of the music, singing and keeping time carefully.

In THE FISHES, the children are arranged as in the pigeon-house; and at the words "swimming," "above," "below," "straight," and "bow," the fishes must make corresponding motions, while the circle that forms the pond goes round singing.

In THE PENDULUM, the children follow each other in a circle, moving one arm before them, like a pendulum, in time to the music, and with a strongly marked motion, while they all sing the song. When one arm is tired, the other can be used for the pendulum.

Let the children also follow one another in a circle to play THE WEATHERCOCK. Beforehand, the points of the compass should be defined in the room, and the children must point, as they sing, "North, South, East, West."

The prettiest of all the plays is THE PEASANT. All join hands and sing, going round in time with the music, when they come to the words, "Look, 'tis so—so does the peasant," they must make the corresponding motion. In the first verse, they make believe, as the children say, to hold up the apron with one hand, and throw the seed with the other. In the second verse, they kneel on one knee at the same words, and make believe hold the corn with one hand and cut with the other. In the third verse, they put the doubled fists at the left shoulder, and make the motion of thrashing. In the fourth verse, they make the motion of holding and shaking a sieve. In the fifth, they kneel on one knee and rest the head in the hand; in the sixth, they jump straight up and down, turning to each point of the compass, till the chorus, "la, la," begins, when each takes his next neighbor for a partner, and they skip round the room.

Some other plays, accompanied by musical words, can be found in the guide-books of European Kindergartens; and the music, with English words, will be shortly published in this country by Ditson, of Boston, to meet the growing demand of Kindergartens.

But the above description of the plays gives no adequate idea of what can be made of them, such as the Kindergartner obtains at the Normal class; for they are much more than bodily exercises. It is wonderful to see what is made of them, in such a Kindergarten as that of Madame Vogler in Berlin, where the conversations before beginning, and in the pauses for rest, call the children's attention to the facts and processes of nature and art, symbolized by the plays.

The words and music are taught very carefully, and the dancing is gentle, so that there may be exhilaration without fatigue.

The object-lessons involved in the plays are those which especially belong to the Kindergarten, because their aim is not so much to open the intellect to science, as to give moral training. The latter is ever to be kept in advance of the former; for it is the *tree of life*, whose fruits—if they are first eaten—will render harmless and salutary those of the tree of knowledge.

I was not unaware of this when I began my own Kindergarten; and the very first thing I did, was to give an object lesson, which was, as I afterwards found, exactly in the spirit of Froebel. When the children were assembled the first day, in my very pleasant room, looking full of expectation, I went forward with a beautiful rose-tree in a little flower-pot, and said, "Come, and I will show you what is beautiful. It is a rose fully blown. Now say the words—all of you—after me; and I said again, 'It is a rose fully blown.'" They all repeated these words with glad voices, and then each following sentence of that beautiful prose hymn of Mrs. Barbauld. I especially noted the smiling eyes and lips, as they repeated,—

"He who made the rose is more beautiful than the rose.

"It is beautiful, but He is beauty."

Another day a basket of roses was handed round to the children; and, when each had one in hand, this recitation was renewed.

After it was over, I said, "What did God make the rose for?" They all smiled, as if conscious of knowing; and one, more courageous than the rest, said, "To give us pleasure;" followed by a dear little utilitarian, who said, "To make rose-water." I added, "Yes; and the rose-water gives us pleasure, too, because it has a sweet smell, and a sweet taste, besides. Is not God very good to give us roses to look at and smell; and to make into rose-water, after they are all faded and fallen to pieces? What is the reason that God makes things to give us pleasure? Could we not have lived very comfortably without flowers?" They answered spontaneously, "Because God loves us." "What else does the dear God give us to make us happy?" Different children answered, and spoke of different flowers, and of other things which gave them pleasure, and thus they were put into a grateful mood, without a word said about the *duty* of gratitude to God; for love of God comes spontaneously, when he is conceived aright, and forecloses the thought of duty. But duty to our fellow-creatures should always be suggested when the heart is overflowing with gratitude to the common Father. I went on asking such questions as "Do *you* love anybody? what do you do to make people happy that you love? what would you like to do with your rose? Do sick people like to have flowers? do you know any sick person? do you like to do the same kind of things God does? do you think God wants you to make your friends happy? and all happy whom he loves?" The roses were then gathered into a shallow basin of water, to be preserved till school should be over, and they could go and bestow them as they had severally suggested; for it is important to make children *do* whatever of kindness they think of, not idly sentimentalize.

Other lessons, on the material origin of the rose, the planting, the process of growth, and even the making of rose-water, opened up; and Mrs.

Barbauld's prose hymns afforded other subjects for similar lessons, as well as whatever other hymns they learned to recite or sing; and I took great care that no hymns should be sung that did not admit of being made intelligible to their hearts and imaginations.

Moral training is effected by taking care in the plays to keep the children in the mood of mutual accommodation, by showing them how this is necessary for the beauty of the play. There is also a great opportunity in the playing, to check all selfish movements, by appeals to sympathy and conscience, which is the presentiment of reason, and forefeeling of moral order, for whose culture material order is indispensable; and order must be kept by the child intentionally, that it may cultivate the intellectual principle of which it is the manifestation. Some plan of play prevents the little creatures from hurting each other, and fancy naturally furnishes the plan,— the mind unfolding itself in fancies, which are easily quickened and led in harmless directions by an adult of any resource. Children delight to personate animals; and a fine genius could not better employ itself than in inventing a great many more plays, setting them to rhythmical words, describing what is to be done. Kindergarten plays are easy intellectual exercises; for to do anything whatever with a thought beforehand, develops the heart or quickens the intelligence; and thought of this kind does not tax intellect, or check physical development, which last must never be sacrificed in the process of education.

There are enough instances of marvellous acquisition in infancy, to show that imbibing with the mind is as natural as with the body, if suitable beverage is put to the lips; but in most cases the mind's power is balanced by instincts of body, which should have priority, if they cannot certainly be in full harmony. The mind can better afford to wait for the maturing of the body, for it survives the body, than the body can afford to wait for the mind; for it is irretrievably stunted, if the nervous energy is not free to stimulate its special organs, at least equally with those of the mind.

There is not, however, any need to sacrifice the culture of either mind or body, but to harmonize them. They can and ought to grow together. They mutually help each other.

CHAPTER V.

THE KINDERGARTNER.

The first requisite to a Kindergarten is, of course, the Kindergartner, fully intelligent of childhood, and thoroughly trained herself in everything that the child is to do.

The first Kindergartner was Froebel himself; who, in the course of a long life, studied into the science of childhood, and worked out a series of artistical exercises, which aim to educate—that is, *draw* forth—the powers of children from a more profound depth than ordinary education respects. But instead of beginning with putting checks upon childish play, he took the hint of his method from this spontaneous activity; and began with genially directing it to a more certainly beautiful effect than it can attain when left to itself. A large part of the art of primary school-teaching hitherto, has consisted in keeping children still, and preventing them from playing.

It was Froebel's wisdom to accept the natural activity of childhood as a hint of the Divine Providence, and to utilize its spontaneous play for education. And it is this which takes away from his system that element of baneful antagonism which school discipline is so apt to excite, and which it is such a misfortune should ever be excited between the young and old. Nothing is worse for the soul, at any period of life, than to be put upon self-defence; for humility is the condition of the growth of mind as well as morals, and ensures that natural self-respect shall not degenerate into a petty wilfulness and self-assertion. The divine impulse of activity in children should not be directly opposed, but accepted and guided into beautiful production, according to the laws of creative order, which the adult has studied out in nature, and genially presents in *playing* with the child.

But such playing is a great art, and founded on the deepest science of nature, within and without; and therefore Froebel never established a Kindergarten without previously preparing Kindergartners by a normal training, which his faithful disciples have scrupulously kept up. And if only genius and love like his own could in one lifetime have discovered the science and worked out the processes of this culture, yet hundreds of pupils of these normal classes have proved, that any fairly gifted, well-educated, genial-tempered young woman, who will devote a reasonable time to training for it, can become a competent Kindergartner.

Nothing short of this will do; for none of the manuals which have been written to guide already trained experts, can supply the place of the living teacher. Written words will not describe the fine gradations of the work, or give an idea of the conversation which is to be constantly had with the children. It would be less absurd to suppose that a person could learn to make watches by reading a description of the manufacture in an encyclopædia, than to suppose a person could learn to educate children by mere formulas.

Indeed, it is *infinitely* less absurd. For a child is not finite mass to be moulded, or a blank paper to be written upon, at another's will. It is a living subject, whose own coöperation—or at least willingness—is to be conciliated and made instrumental to the end in view. Would a Cremona violin be put into the hands of a person ignorant of music, to be tuned and made to discourse divine harmonies? How is it, then, that the "harp of a thousand strings"—which God puts into the hands of every mother, in perfect tune—is so recklessly committed, first to ignorant girl-nurses, and then to the least educated teachers? Looking at children's first schools, it would seem that anybody is thought skilful enough to begin a child's education! It takes a long apprenticeship to learn to play on the instrument with seven strings, in order to bring out music. But it is stupidly thought that anybody can play on the greater instrument, whose strings thrill with pleasure or pain, and discourse good or evil, as they are touched wisely or unwisely!

Froebel struck the key-note of the music of the spheres, which human life is destined to become, when he announced, as a first principle, that the well-thought-out wisdom of the ideal mother's love is the science of education; and that this science of sciences is founded on self-knowledge; by which he did not mean (any more than did Socrates, or that older sage who engraved "know thyself" upon the temple of Delphi) individual idiosyncrasy, but the very self which Jesus Christ said all men must *become*, when he set a little child in the midst, and declared that no one could enter his kingdom, that did not *become* as *one*; and when, another time, he called and blessed little children, because, as he said, of such was the kingdom of heaven; and again, more significantly still, when he warned from "*offending* (it might be better rendered *perverting*) these little ones; *because*," as he added, "*their spirits do always behold the face of my Father who is in heaven.*" To know the soul before it has been warped by individual caprice and circumstance, is the science of sciences, on which is to be founded the art of arts; viz., that of educating the child so that its individuality may develop, not destroy, its sense of universal relations. And here I must pause to say, that it is simply astonishing that when most of us believe, as our religion, that Jesus Christ embodied in himself the wisdom, as well as love, and even power of God,—"without measure,"—his words about children are passed over with so little inquiry into the depths of their *meaning*. What can it mean—that their spirits always behold the face of the Father—short of the very philosophy of Gioberti,—that the newly-created soul commences its consciousness in the eternal world, with a reciprocal vision of God *remembered in the heart* through life, and constituting the divine term of conscience, which is the CONSTANT, while the human term is of only fitful growth. As Wordsworth says,—

> "Our Life's Star
> Hath had elsewhere its setting,
>   And cometh from afar!
>   Not in entire forgetfulness
>   And not in utter nakedness,
> But trailing clouds of glory do we come
>   From God who is our home.
> Heaven lies about us in our infancy!
> Shades of the prison-house begin to close
>   Upon the growing boy,
> But he beholds the light and whence it flows;
>   He sees it *in his joy*:
> The youth, who daily from the East
> Must travel, still is nature's priest,

> And by the vision splendid
> Is on his way attended."

But Froebel does not, like Wordsworth, make it strictly inevitable, however it may have hitherto been common, that

> "The man perceives it die away
> And fade into the light of common day;"

for he teaches that the parental sympathy and instruction of those adults who have attained

> "The faith that looks through death
> In years that bring the philosophic mind"

should intervene; which is just Kindergarten culture; preserving the heart's vision of the truths that

> "We are toiling all our lives to find"

unshadowed; while the organs of the human mind gradually bring to bear God's manifestation in nature, which, point by point, forms the human understanding, by making an intellectual consciousness of what the heart knows.

Because the science of education is the analysis and gauging of love by intellect, Froebel sought the true form of the art of education in the method of the mother's love, which he studied out with a philosophic earnestness. Not that any mother could *tell* him the secret. It cannot be put into formulas, nor does it come by intuition into the scientific form in which a Kindergartner needs to have it. Froebel, in watching the mother, saw that she was "led in a way she knew not." But he divined the meaning of that way, and its issues, and gives it to the Kindergartner.

The beginning of a child's life is its learning the fact and uses of its body. Here, as everywhere, human action blindly gropes for knowledge. The child cannot even find the breast to suck, but sucks what is nearest, compelling the mother to give it the breast by automatic motions which she understands; or by cries which awaken her heart. Gradually these reciprocal instincts open upon the child the first thing it knows; namely, that it is dependent for the means of life. For a child knows, in its heart, for a long time before it reflects and gets the thought, that not in itself, but outside of itself, is the source of its life. Of course, it is bodily life merely that it seeks at first, trying to incorporate the without with the within by eating every thing; the organs for this action on the outward world being first developed. But if it is regularly fed and kept comfortable, the eye will be satisfied with seeing, the ear with hearing, the hand with handling.

Now it is no less the instinct of the mother to make the baby's body the first plaything, than to feel its own body is the first pleasure of the child. To use its organs in play is the first action in which the voluntary combines with the instinctive animal impulse.

The first distinctive human intelligence a child *expresses*, is the recognition of its mother's smile. Its higher life begins in the reciprocation of that smile. *No mere animal smiles!* The mother's heart also goes to meet the child's faith with vocal expressions of tender joy; the heart of the child is awakened by tones which emparadise it, and it answers by like tones. There is nothing among the lower animals like this conversation of mother and child, by looks and tones, emparadising both. By and by, it notices light and colors, and begins to play with its hands and feet.

Hence the most characteristic work of Froebel is "The Mother's Cosseting Songs." In this imperfect world, mothers are not always true to ideal motherhood; but ignorance, and often indolence, and other forms of self-indulgence, superinducing stupidity,—even a tyrannous sense of property in the child, and sometimes mere timidity, interferes. And, in general, Froebel saw how little most mothers reflect on the great work they are doing when they play with their children. He wished them to study into the laws they are obeying, in order to discover their scope and meaning, that they may be able to supplement with thought the short-comings of their too often spoilt instincts. Mothers taught him more than they knew themselves; and he repaid the debt by telling them what they taught him in these "Cosseting Songs," which he gathered from many lips and brought together for the enriching of all.

First may be seen in the pictured illustrations which accompany the songs, that the plays are merely the sympathetic furtherance of the child's own motions. The mother enjoys the sight of her baby kicking up its little legs, fumbling its little hands, and enjoying its bodily existence generally; and she sympathizingly intervenes, and draws the child to forget itself in its heart-sense of her sympathetic presence. She feeds the instinctive putting forth of its own joy, the first form of its faith, with the expression of her joy; and thus the heart grows with the body, and the mind opens to expect boundless love, which it reciprocates without reserve. A healthy child

"Loves whate'er it looks upon."

If it is not happy and loving, it is the condemnation of its environment. Some one in relation with it, perhaps more than one, has failed to show the necessary love; and "better were it for such," as Jesus Christ has said "that a millstone were hung about their necks, and they were cast into the uttermost depths of the sea." If these words mean any thing,—and who will dare say they are mere rhetoric?—then let us take care that we do not rush into the work of education, without being sure that we shall not do so immense a mischief; and let mothers see to it, that they do not put their children into the care of persons who do not combine love and knowledge of childhood in measures not to be expected of the common run of children's nurses and primary teachers.

Not only because every mother is not an ideal mother, but because sometimes children are consigned, by inevitable circumstance, to other nursing than a wise mother's, such a manual as the "Cosseting Songs" is indispensable *to instruct nurses*.

And nurses ought always to be instructed. When Froebel was in Hamburg, he received nurses into normal training. Both mothers and nurses brought their infants of six months old to his house, and he taught them how to play with—without fatiguing—them, by carefully respecting those indications of pleasure and pain which are the child's only means of communication.

And as lectures on *child-nature* are a part of the Kindergarten training, those preparing to be children's nurses, even to this day, are admitted to the Hamburg training-school, which was not relinquished when Froebel died, but is now instructed by the best teachers of the Volks-Kindergartens, who go into it by turns. It has its sessions in the evenings; and the normal pupils pay for their instruction, at least in part, by assisting in the morning in the Volks-Kindergarten, which forms also an important part of their training.

But at all events, there can be no adequate Kindergarten culture anywhere, unless a specific normal training is constantly kept up to supply the ever-increasing demand which tends to outgo the supply, especially when nurses are admitted, as at Hamburg.

Having thus indicated the source whence must be drawn the Kindergarten culture, it is not our purpose to attempt the impossible, by stating it abstractly; for a series of abstractions is more apt to conceal than to reveal a living science. No book can train a Kindergartner, but only at best serve as a convenient reminder to educated experts, and instruct parents that there is one necessary condition of their children's receiving the benefit of Kindergarten culture; viz., a thoroughly educated Kindergartner.

And this may be obtained even in America, from a lady of *the apostolic succession*; a pupil of the training-school of the Baroness Marienholtz, of Berlin, who has devoted her talents, her fortune, the prestige of her rank, and her personal services, to spread the art of her revered master on the continent of Europe. Miss Kriege not only has studied a year in this training-school, but all the while frequented the Kindergarten of Madame Vogler, as observer and assistant; and,—together with her mother, a lady who is the equal of the Baroness Marienholtz in every thing but the fortune which enables the latter to teach without price,—combines every qualification, with enthusiasm, for the spread of a method of education that unquestionably has a great future in this country, inasmuch as it makes a true base to the grand harmonies of our national constitution.

As one feature of the normal class is a series of lectures on *the being of the child*, which are given on one day of the week, it would be desirable that Madame Kriege should admit mothers and sisters who have no intention of making teaching their vocation, but who may thus understand and be able to co-operate in spirit with the Kindergartner, in the education of the children; for it is a great hindrance to the Kindergarten when it is not understood at home. All the educators of the child should understand each other, and co-operate, if the highest results are to be attained.

CHAPTER VI.

KINDERGARTEN OCCUPATIONS.

There is a kind of thing done in Kindergarten, which retains the best characteristics of childish play, and yet assumes the serious form of occupation.

Fancy-work, if Froebel's method be strictly followed, is the best initiation of industry; for it can serve to a perfect intellectual training.

Childish play has all the main characteristics of art, inasmuch as it is the endeavor to "conform the shows of things to the desires of the mind,"—Bacon's definition of poetry. A child at play is histrionic. He personates characters, with costume and mimic gesture. He also undertakes to represent whatever thing interests his mind by embodiment of it in outward form. Advantage is taken of this, by Froebel, to initiate exquisite manipulation, in several different materials; a veritable artistic work, which trains the imagination to use, and develops the understanding to the appreciation of beauty, symmetry, or order,—"Heaven's first law."

Froebel's first two Gifts, as they are called, are a box of colored worsted balls, and a box containing the cube, the sphere, and the cylinder. These two Gifts belong more especially to the nursery series, and were published some years since in Boston, with little books of rhymes, and suggestions for playing with babies.

But they can be used, in some degree, in the Kindergarten: the first, to give lessons on the harmonies of colors; and the second, to call attention to fundamental differences of form.

It is possible, however, to omit these, and begin a Kindergarten with the Third Gift, which is a little wooden box, containing eight cubes of an inch dimension.

The first plays with these blocks, especially if the children are very young, will be to make what Froebel calls forms of life; that is, chairs, tables, columns, walls, tanks, stables, houses, &c. Everybody conversant with children knows how easily they will "make believe," as they call it, all these different forms, out of any materials whatever; and are most amused, when the materials to be transformed by their personifying and symbolizing fancy are few, for so much do children enjoy the exercise of imagination, that they find it more amusing to have simple forms, which they can "make believe,"—first to be one thing, and then another,—than to have elaborately carved columns, and such like materials, for building. There is nothing in life more charming to a spectator, than to see this shaping fancy of children, making everything of nothing, and scorning the bounds of probability, and even of possibility. It is a prophecy of the unending dominion which man was commanded, at his creation, to have over nature; and gives meaning to the parable of the Lord God's bringing all creatures before Adam, that he might give them their names.

Wordsworth felicitously describes, in that ode which he calls "Intimations of Immortality in Childhood," this victorious play of—

> "The seer blest,
> On whom those truths do rest,
> Which we are toiling all our lives to find."

> "Behold the child among his new-born blisses;
> A six years' darling of a pigmy size;
> See where, mid work of his own hand, he lies,
> Fretted by sallies of his mother's kisses,
> With light upon him from his father's eyes!
> See at his feet some little plan or chart,
> Some fragment of his dream of human life,
> Shaped by himself with newly learned art,—
>   A wedding or a festival,
>   A mourning or a funeral;
> And this hath now his heart,
> And unto this he frames his song.
> Then he will fit his tongue
> To dialogues of business, love, or strife;

> But it will not be long
> Ere this be thrown aside,
> And with new joy and pride,
> The little actor cons another part;
> Filling from time to time his humourous stage
> With all the persons down to palsied age
> That life brings with her in her equipage."

That this is a literal picture, every mother knows; and, in this childish play, there is all the subjective part of a genuine work of art; the effort being to dramatize, or embody in form, the inward fancy, no less than in the case of the most mature and successful artist. The child seizes whatever materials are at hand to give objectivity to what is within; and he is only baffled in the effect, because he is not developed enough in understanding, and has not knowledge enough to discover or appreciate means appropriate to his ends. It is for the adult to show him that the universe is a magazine of materials given to the human race, wherewith each is to build an image of God's creative wisdom, into which he shall inwardly grow by the very act of accomplishing this destiny.

As the child is satisfied at first with a symbolical representation of his inward thought, a row of chairs and footstools, arranged in a line, makes a railroad to his imagination; and no less a row of cubes, one being piled on another for the engine.

In using the blocks in a Kindergarten, the child at first is left to his own spontaneity, as much as possible; but the teacher is to suggest means of carrying out whatever plan or idea he has. What is cultivating about the exercise is, that the child makes or receives a plan, and then executes it; has a thought, and embodies it in a form.

But something more can be done with the blocks. They can be made symbolical of the personages and objects of a story. Thus even with the eight blocks, five may be a flock of sheep, one the shepherd, one a wolf who is seen in the distance, and who comes to steal a sheep, and one the shepherd's dog who is to defend the sheep against the wolf.

When all the Gifts come to be used, much more complicated dramas may be represented. The teacher should set an example; as, for instance, thus: "I am going to build a light-house, so;" (she piles up some blocks and leaves openings near the top, which she says are) "the lantern part where the lights are put;" near the light-house are a number of blocks, rather confusedly laid together, of which she says, "These are rocks, which are very dangerous for ships, but which are scarcely ever seen, because the water dashes over them, especially when there is a storm, or when the night is dark; and that is the reason the light-house is put here. Whenever sailors see a light-house, they know there is danger where it stands; and so they steer their ships away from the place. Look here! here is a ship" (and she constructs with other blocks something which she calls a ship, or schooner, or sloop, representing respectively the number of masts which characterize each kind of vessel), "and there is a pilot standing upon it who has seen the light-house, and is turning the ship another way."

Having built her story, she will now call upon the children to build something. Some will imitate her; others will have plans of their own. As soon as one has finished, he or she must hold up a hand; and the teacher will call upon as many as there is time for, to explain their constructions. There is no better way for a teacher to learn what is in children, their variety of mental temperament and imagination, than by this playing with blocks. Some will be prosaic and merely imitative; some will show the greatest confusion, and the most fantastic operations of mind; others, the most charming fancies; and others, inventive genius. But there will always be improvement, by continuing the exercise; and it is a great means of development into self-subsistence and continuity of thought.

But to return to Froebel's Third Gift, consisting of eight blocks. In making things with the blocks, a great deal is to be said about setting them accurately upon each other, and upon the squares drawn on the table (if it is so painted). I was both amused and instructed, when I was in Hamburg, by seeing a little table full of children taking a first lesson in making two chairs, by piling three blocks on each other for the back, and putting one in front for the seat; the Kindergartner going round so seriously to see if each block was adjusted exactly, and stood squarely. When, at length, the chairs were done, the children took hold of hands, and recited, simultaneously with the Kindergartner, a verse of poetry; and then sang it. I could not understand the words; but the conversation, while they were making the chairs, had helped the several children's fancy to seat their fathers, mothers, or grandparents, or some other favorite friends, in them; each child having been asked for whom he wished to make his chairs, which developed a good deal of the domestic circumstances. None of the class was more than four years old. But the most important use of the eight blocks is to lead the children through a series of symmetrical forms, which Froebel calls forms of beauty.

As a preparation for this work, the children are questioned, till they understand which is the right, and which the left side of the cube made by the eight blocks; which the front, and which the back side; which the upper, and which the under side; and are able to describe a cube by its dimensions; also to know how to divide the whole cube into two, four, or eight parts; how to divide the length, how the breadth, and how the height, into two parts,—lessons of analysis sufficiently amusing, and giving precision to their use of words.

Dividing the height, they get a simple fundamental form; and the four blocks taken off can be arranged around the others symmetrically.

For instance: tell them, first, to take an inch cube and place it in front of the square that the four lower blocks make, so that one-half shall be on one block, and the other half on the other; then tell them to take another small cube, and place it opposite, in the same way, one-half on one cube, and the other half on the other. Already they will find the figure is symmetrical, or, as they may phrase it, even. Then tell them to put a cube on the right hand of the fundamental figure in the same way as before, and then another opposite on the left side; and the figure will be still more symmetrical.

When this has been recognized all round, tell them to move the front block just half a block to the right; then the opposite one half a block to the left; then the right-hand block half a block farther back; and, on the opposite side, the left-hand block half a block towards the front. This will make again a symmetrical form. Again, they may be told to move the front block half a block farther to the right; and then move the opposite one to the left, and so on,—which will make another figure. Their attention must be drawn to the fact that always—if the symmetry is to be retained—all four of the movable blocks must be moved; demonstrating to the eyes, by otherwise placing them, that symmetry is more pleasing than confusion, and order than disorder.

In going on, through the large number of forms which are given in the manuals of Madame Rongé and the Baroness Marienholtz, for the convenience of the Kindergartners, the children can be asked in turn to suggest rules for new figures, and then directed how to apply the rule, and adjust each of the four blocks to make a symmetry. Often, a form of the series given, is anticipated; but, if no suggestion is made by the children, the Kindergartner must choose, and ask if so and so would not be pretty. But in no case must the engraved forms be given as a pattern. Imitation is mechanical, and children soon tire of working by patterns; while to work from a rule, whether it is suggested by another, or is one's own fancy, will keep up the interest a long while, and stimulate invention; for it is real intellectual work, though less abstract than geometry.

The great secret of the charm of working out symmetrical forms is, that the mind is created to make, like the divine mind. "God geometrizes," says Plato; and therefore man geometrizes. The generation of forms by crystallization, and by vegetable and animal organization, follows the law of polarity, which is alike the law of the human and the mode of the divine creation. It was amusing to hear a little child cry out, "I cannot find an opposite;" and, when another said, "No matter, take this," reply, "But then it will not make anything."

In going through the series of forms, made first by the eight blocks, then by those of the Fourth Gift, and afterwards by the larger number of the Fifth and Sixth Gifts, the child comes, by being led perpetually to put down *opposites*, in order to make symmetry, to learn the value of the law of polarization, which obtains alike in thought, and in the created universe.

But, besides the boxes of solids, there are boxes of triangles, one of equilateral, one of right angle, and two of isosceles triangles—one acute and one obtuse—affording means for an infinity of forms of beauty; so that this amusement of making symmetrical forms is not exhausted in the whole four years of the Kindergarten course.

The same principle of polarity is brought out in the combination of colors, as well as of forms.

In weaving bookmarks and mats, with strips of different colored papers, the series of forms becomes more attractive by observing the harmonies of color. The children are taught, by the colored balls of the First Gift, to distinguish the primary and secondary colors, and to arrange them harmoniously. Children acquire very soon a very exquisite taste in color, and, if carefully called to attend to harmonies, detect an incongruity at once.

Calkins, of New York, has published sheets of diagrams, if they may be so called, of the harmonies of colors.

The Kindergartner, while at the training-school, gets a series of several hundred woven forms, to relieve her from the fatigue of constantly inventing, when she is full of care. But children soon begin to invent of themselves, and are recreated—not fatigued—by it. This weaving may be turned to much account for innumerable ornamental articles which the children are delighted to make, in order to have something of their own, to give to their friends, at Christmas, New Year's, and birthdays. Our woodcut gives the beginning of the series of woven forms. Children of three years old can begin these; and those of five will make beautiful things. But a series of forms may perhaps be most easily begun by little children, by sewing colored worsted threads into pricked paper.

One essential furniture of the Kindergarten is paper ruled in squares of a sixteenth of an inch, which can be done wherever paper is ruled. Every child should have a piece of this paper, pricked in the crossings of the squares, and be taught to use the needle and colored thread, so as first to make parallel lines, then diagonals, then right angles, then squares; and then other more complex but still symmetrical figures.

This squared paper may also be used to teach pricking, first at the crossings of the lines, preparing sheets for sewing, and then making a series by pricking symmetrical forms; following the same general law as produced beauty with the blocks and triangular planes.

Also, simultaneously with these occupations, the children should be induced to draw, by means of this squared paper. A very small child can be taught to use the pencil, so far as to draw a line of an eighth of an inch over the blue line, or the water-mark of the squared paper. Immediately these lines must be so drawn as to correspond and make forms; and it is perfectly wonderful to the child himself, to find how, by following the rules given, he goes straight on to make the most complicated forms and beautiful designs. When I was in Dresden, I bought of Madame Marquadt hundreds of drawings made in series by children between three and seven years of age, where no stroke was longer than an eighth of an inch. I was told that every one was the *invention* of some child; for only inventions were carefully preserved.

But another manipulation must not be forgotten; viz., the folding of paper.

Here, a square piece of paper, of four or five inches, is given to the child, who had previously been exercised in building with solids, in making forms with sticks, and in pea-work; which last is done by having sharp-pointed sticks of various lengths, and constructing squares, triangles, and the frames of chairs, and other articles of furniture, uniting the sticks by means of dried peas, soaked in water. (See woodcut.)

As the sticks and peas were used to teach the properties of geometrical lines and points, which they clumsily represent, so the square of paper can be used to develop ideas of surface and geometrical planes; without, however, using any abstract geometrical language.

Folding paper develops the value of the law of polarity, just as all other symmetrical work does; but there is the additional charm to children, of making, by means of this folded paper, a multitude of forms of life as well as of beauty; involving a great instruction. For always the folding begins with nothing but a square piece of paper, which, by following their thought, is made into hundreds of beautiful forms; and thus they learn to respect in themselves the power of thought applied to work, which is nothing less than *creative*. By cutting off a piece of the folded paper, while still it is folded, a new series of forms can be made, of unimagined symmetrical forms, which the children, when they unfold the paper, are electrified to find they have caused; and, with the pieces cut out, they can also enrich the figures with new varieties of symmetrical beauty.

I have seen, in one of the Kindergartens, five hundred different figures made out of the simple square, variously folded and cut. The attention of the children should be called to the fact of this endless capacity of development of the simplest and most uninteresting form, by the exercise of human ingenuity, acting according to law. Thus they will realize that beauty is not an outward thing, but an inward power, which they exert.

This cutting and folding of paper can only be learned in a Kindergarten training-school. It cannot be described in a book.

Modelling is the highest form of manipulation of solids, and one which is very fascinating to children, who often make forms with mud and snow in their out-door play.

The material, whether clay, rice, wax, or whatever else may be employed, must be previously prepared, and always kept in a plastic state.

Clay is the least expensive material, but it must always be kept wet, and it is cold to the hands. Wax, prepared with oil, is more expensive, but far cleaner than clay; and it has the advantage of preserving the forms moulded, while the clay shrinks and cracks when it dries.

The material being prepared, each child is supplied either with a small flat board, slate, cloth, or strong paper, to cover the part of the table used; a small blunt elastic knife, and a portion of the plastic material. The child is first left to pursue the bent of its own inclinations, generally the roller and the ball are the first objects attempted. In their formation the child finds great delight. Irregular forms are, however, the easiest. The children are encouraged to imitate birds' nests, baskets, candlesticks, and various fruits: apples, pears, strawberries, also some vegetables, and especially flowers;— whenever it is possible let them have the natural objects before them. Afterwards models of animals *couchant* are given for imitation; and they are encouraged to make parts of the human figure,—fingers, hands, ears, noses, for which they have models in each other. I have known a boy not twelve years old, who would take an engraved head, and mould one by it, in which the likeness would be remarkable;—he used wax and a pin.

To make forms from the hint of an engraving, is a little above imitation; and it is to be remembered that we do not wish the children to stop with imitations. Let them go on and invent forms, beautiful vases, pitchers, &c. When they begin to make heads and human figures, a teacher, who understands the principles of drawing, can bring to their notice the proportions of the human figure and face found in nature, which make ideal beauty. Many a heaven-destined sculptor will find himself out, in the Kindergarten.

In Germany, at the quadrennial meetings of the Froebel Union, it is the custom to carry specimens of the children's work in all these kinds. A series of each kind is made up by taking the best work of all the children. The six meetings which have already taken place, have all been signalized by impressing upon the commissioners of education of some State, the value of Froebel's culture to the interests of art,—fine and mechanical,—followed by its adoption. And yet its value to art is of secondary importance to its influence on character, which must needs be lifelong,—leading away from temptation, and delivering from evil, the activity secured to the production of use and beauty.

In America, where the excitements of opportunity are literally infinite, the importance of training the speculative mind and immense energy of the people to law, order, beauty, and love (which are all one in the last analysis), is incalculable; and that it can be done most easily and certainly by beginning with the child's mind while he is still "beholding the face of the Father in heaven" with his heart, no one who has ever faithfully tried Kindergarten culture will doubt.

MORAL AND RELIGIOUS EXERCISES.

Harmonious development is Froebel's idea. Hence, although the physical should never be sacrificed, and comes first into view, in the scheme of Kindergarten culture, it is not to be exclusive. Children grow in stature and physical force, all the better for having their hearts and minds opened in the beginning. It is desirable to have a child become conscious of right and wrong, in reference to eating and drinking, quite early; though temptation to excess should be removed, as a general thing, by giving them simple wholesome food. In any case where children may not go home at noon, and there is a luncheon, some simple fruit, like apples or grapes, together with milk biscuits, or plain bread and butter, make the best repast, satisfying hunger, and not stimulating the palate unduly. I am sometimes shocked at the kind of luncheon children bring to the Kindergarten, it shows such lamentable ignorance of physiological laws. The practical value of the beautiful symbol of the origin of evil, which stands as the first word of the sacred volume, is enhanced, by its having the form in which temptation first assails the child. No deeper interpretation of it is foreclosed by our presenting it at first, to children, just as it stands. The forbidden fruit is that which will hurt the child; *i. e.*, give it the disease which by and by may make death a merciful release from pains intolerable to bear. Serpents have no higher function than eating; but human beings live to know and love and do good, and so ought not to eat everything that is pleasant to the eyes,—but to stop, as Eve did not, and inquire whether it is God or the mere animal which is man's proper adviser. Our appetite is the serpent, our thought is from God. A child understands all this very early, if it is thus simply presented; and it suggests the beginning of his moral life. The lesson can soon be generalized. Whatever wrong things he is tempted to do, whatever his conscience tells him not to do, is "forbidden fruit;" his desire to do it is the serpent, and if he falls, it is the old folly of Eve, who preferred the advice of the lower being to the command of God, always given in the Conscience.

I have known a child, to whom this story was early read and interpreted, to whom it seemed to become a "guard angelic" over her life. The moral nature responded to it at once, and a suggestion that a desire was perhaps the voice of the serpent, was always quite enough to arouse the guardian angel—Conscience—to a watch and ward of the severest character. It precluded the necessity of present punishment and the fear of future retribution, (with which a child should never be terrified.)

There is such a thing as making children, I will not say too conscientious, but too conscious; and this is often done by well-meaning parents and teachers, who make them look upon themselves personally as objects of God's pleasure or displeasure. This will be avoided by using a symbol, like the story of Adam and Eve, which touches the imagination, and saves them from the reactions of personal pique. A judicious teacher, who knows how to paraphrase as she reads, and to skip what is mere prosaic statement, (and no one who cannot do this, is fit to read to children,) can make use of many other passages of the Old and New Testament, and of "Pilgrim's Progress," to give to children the whole doctrine of religious self-control, and inspire them to the highest moral issues.

Spiritual life, strictly speaking, can only be *prepared for* by the *best* education. Its characteristic and essence consists in that action of the heart and reason which does not come from human prompting. But it *can* be prepared for, by awakening in the child such an aspiration and felt necessity for virtue, as well as general idea of God, as makes prayer to the Father of Spirits spontaneous and inevitable. I am in the habit of speaking of God to children as the Giver of love and goodness, and of the power of thought and action, rather than as the Creator of the outward world, and have found that the tyrannizing unity of the soul's instinct did the rest.

In what is called religious education, teachers often do great harm, with the best intentions, to finely strung moral organizations. Encouragement to good should altogether predominate over warning and fault-finding. It is often better, instead of blaming a child for short-coming, or even wrong-doing, to pity and sympathize, and, in a hopeful voice, speak of it as something which the child did not mean to do, or at least was sorry for as soon as done; suggesting at the same time, perhaps, how it can be avoided another time. Above all things, an invariable rule in moral education is not to throw a child upon self-defence. The movement towards defending one's self and making excuses, is worse than almost any act of overt wrong. Let the teacher always appear as the friend who is saving or helping the child out of evil, rather than as the accuser, judge, or executioner. Another principle should be, not to confound or put upon the same level the trespasses against the by-laws of the Kindergarten, made for the teacher's convenience, and those against the moral laws of the universe. The desirableness of the by-laws that we make for our convenience can be shown at times when the children are all calm, and their attention can be drawn to the subject; and if these regulations are broken, all that is necessary will be to ask if it is kind and loving to do such things? But it must never be forgotten that natural conscience always suffers when artificial duties are imposed. Hence the immoral effect of formality and superstition.

In a well-regulated Kindergarten there should be no punishments, but an understanding should be had with parents that sometimes the child is to be sent home for a day, or at least for some hours. The curtailment of the Kindergarten will generally prove an effectual restraint upon disorder, and it will not be necessary to repeat the penalty in a school year.

But I shall say no more upon moral and religious exercises, Mrs. Mann having treated this part of the subject so exhaustively. It is to be remembered, however, that she had in her school children who had strayed much farther from the kingdom of heaven than those who will generally make up the Kindergarten. But she shows the *spirit* that should pervade all that is done to children at all times.

> I saw, in observing the Kindergartens of Germany, that there was great moral education involved in the mutual consideration of each other, which the children learn to practise, in order to make the plays beautiful; and also in the constant idea kept before them, of making beautiful things for the purpose of giving pleasure to their parents and other friends, by giving them away on birthdays and Christmas and New-Year's Days. Moral education does not come by the hearing of the ear, but by generous life.

CHAPTER VIII.

OBJECT LESSONS.

I now come to Object Lessons, which should begin simultaneously with all the above exercises; for mental exercises are not only compatible with physical health, but necessary to it. The brain is not to be overstrained in childhood, but it is to be used. Where it is left to itself, and remains uncultivated, it shrinks, and that is disease. A child is not able to direct its own attention; it needs the help of the adult in the unfolding of the mind, no less than in the care of its body. Lower orders of animals can educate themselves, that is, develop in themselves their one power. As the animals rise in the scale of being, they are related more or less to their progenitors and posterity, and require social aid. But the human being, whose beatitude is "the communion of the just," is so universally related, that he cannot go alone at all. He is entirely dependent at first, and never becomes independent of those around him, any further than he has been so educated and trained by his relations with them, as to rise into union with God. And this restores him again to communion with his fellow-beings, as a beneficent Power among its peers.

The new method of education gives a gradual series of exercises, continuing the method of Nature. It cultivates the senses, by giving them the work of discriminating colors, sounds, &c.; sharpens perception by leading children to describe accurately the objects immediately around them.

Objects themselves, rather than the verbal descriptions of objects, are presented to them. The only way to make words expressive and intelligible, is to associate them sensibly with the objects to which they relate. Children must be taught to translate things into words, before they can translate words into things. Words are secondary in nature; yet much teaching seems to proceed on the principle that these are primary, and so they become mere counters, and children are brought to hating study, and the discourse of teachers, instead of thirsting for them. To look at objects of nature and art, and state their colors, forms, and properties of various kinds, is no painful strain upon the mind. It is just what children spontaneously do when they are first learning to talk. It is a continuation of learning to talk. The object-teacher confines the child's attention to one thing, till all that is obvious about it is described; and then asks questions, bringing out much that children, left to themselves, would overlook, suggesting words when necessary, to enable them to give an account of what they see. It is the action of the mind upon real things, together with clothing perceptions in words, which really cultivates; while it is not the painful strain upon the brain which the study of a book is. To translate things into words, is a more agreeable and a very different process from translating words into things, and the former exercise should precede the latter. If the mind is thoroughly exercised in wording its perceptions, words will in their turn suggest the things, without painful effort, and memory have the clearness and accuracy of perception. On the other hand words will never be used without feeling and intelligence. Then, to read a book will be to know all of reality that is in it.

I am desirous to make a strong impression on this point, because, to many persons, I find object-teaching seems the opposite of teaching! They say that to play with things, does not give habits of study. They think that to commit to memory a page of description about a wild duck, for instance, is better than to have the wild duck to look at, leading the child to talk about it, describe it, and inquire into its ways and haunts! They do not see that this study of the things themselves exercises the perception, and picturesque memory, which is probably immortal, certainly perennial, while the written description only exercises the verbal memory. Verbal memory is not to be despised; but it is a consequence, and should never be the substitute for picturesque memory. It is the picturesque memory only which is creative.

There is another and profound reason why words should follow, and not precede things, in a child's memory. It will have a tendency to preclude the unconscious sophistry which takes the place of real logic in so many minds; and at all events will give the power to detect sophistry; for it necessitates the mind to demand an image, or an idea, for every word. It gives the habit of thinking things and principles, instead of thinking words merely;—of looking through rhetoric after truth and reality. There is nothing perhaps which would conduce more to sound morality and earnestness of character, in this country, than that object-teaching, as proposed in Mr. Sheldon's "ELEMENTARY INSTRUCTION," should pervade the primary schools. It would require a volume to go into object-teaching, in such detail as to serve as a manual for teachers; and happily the work of Mr. Sheldon's, just named, precludes the necessity of my doing so. It is published broadcast over our northern States; and every teacher, especially every Kindergarten teacher, should procure it, and give days and nights to the study of it, until its methods and matter are completely mastered. I have one or two exceptions to take, in respect to it myself, as will be seen in the sequel; yet I consider it not only an invaluable manual, but that it goes far to supply the place of the training school for teachers on the Pestalozzian plan, "for whose use I believe it was primarily intended."

Object-teaching should precede as well as accompany the process of learning to read. In Germany, even outside of Kindergarten, *thinking schools* have long preceded *reading schools*, and yet learning to read German, in which every sound is represented by a different letter, and every letter has one sound, cultivates the classifying powers, as learning to read English cannot. With children whose vernacular is English, it is absolutely injurious to the mind to be taught to read the first thing. I must speak of the reasons of this in another place, my purpose here being to show that object-teaching is necessary, in order to make word-teaching, whether by teacher's discourse, or by the reading of books, a means of culture at any period.

Every child should have the object to examine, and in turn each should say what is spontaneous. Out of their answers series of questions will be suggested to the teacher, who should also be prepared with her own series of questions,—questions full of answers.

The first generalization to which children should be led is into the animate and inanimate,—what lives and what exists without manifestation of life. The next generalization will be into mineral, vegetable, animal, and personal.

But you can begin with chairs, tables, paper, cloth, &c., coming as soon as possible to natural objects. Mrs. Agassiz's "First Lesson in Natural History" is an excellent hint. Sea anemones, star-fishes, clams, and oysters are easily procured. If sea anemones, taken into a bottle of salt water, clinging to stones, look like mere mosses at first, on the second day it is pretty certain, that in their desire for food they will spread themselves out, displaying their inward parts in the most beautiful manner. Every child in the class should have his turn at the object, if there are not objects enough for each,—should tell what he sees, and be helped to words to express himself. This, I must repeat, is the true way of learning the meaning of words; and leaves impressions, which no dictionary, with its periphrases and mere approximations to synonymes can give. Let a child himself hammer out some substance with a mallet, and he will never forget the meaning of malleable; and so of other words. As far as possible we should always use Saxon words, but it is the words that come from the Latin and Greek, which it is most necessary to teach the meaning of; and they should be taught by things themselves, which have them for names or qualities.

A good linguist will have an advantage here, by being able to trace the words through the original language up to nature; for every word is, in the last analysis, either a picture, whose original in nature is its definition, or a poem, which can be recognized by the general imagination. A child whose vernacular is English will easily see that a *bit* is something bitten off, and so is smaller than the mouth; but that *morsel* means a bit is not so obvious to one who does not know that *morsus*, also, is the perfect participle of the Latin verb for bite. That *acute* means *sharp* is plainer to a child who knows that *acu* is the Latin for needle.

No time is lost which is given to this definition of words by the objects of nature and art, from which, or from whose attributes, words are derived. In words are fossilized the sciences, that is, the knowledge mankind has already attained of nature; and he who understands all the words in use, would know all that is known, nay, much that has been once known and long forgotten. But the study of objects not only gives significance to words, it educates the senses, and produces the habit of original attention and investigation of nature. These do not come of themselves, as we see in the instance of country children, who are ignorant of what is around them, because left to grow up among the objects of nature, without having their attention called to things in their minutiæ, or their relations in extensu; nor led to clothe with words their perceptions, impressions, and reasonings.

Besides Mr. Sheldon's "Elementary Instruction," there is the "Child's Book of Nature," by Worthington Hooker, in three parts, which will be a great help to an object-teacher. It is published by the Harpers, and is the very best introduction of children to flowers.[D] Mrs. Mann's "Flower People" is also full of facts, carefully studied out. This is a charming book for children to read in, when they shall come to read. It is a great pity that the latest edition, published by Ticknor and Fields in 1862, is not illustrated by the flowers spoken of. But perhaps these may be lithographed, and published in a card-case, to accompany it. Both the science and cultivation of flowers comes very naturally into the Kindergarten.

The greatest difficulty about object-teaching is, that it requires personal training, and wide-awake attention in teachers, of a character much more thorough than they commonly have. When it shall become general, as it certainly must, it will no longer be supposed that any ordinary person who can read and write, and is obliged to do something for a living, will be thought fit to keep a school for small children! The present order of things will be reversed. Ordinary persons, with limited acquirements, will be obliged to confine themselves to older pupils, who are able to study books and only need to have some one to set their lessons and hear them recited; while persons of originality and rich culture will be reserved to discover and bring out the various genius and faculty which God has sown broadcast in the field of the race, and which now so often runs into the rank vegetation of vice, or wastes into deserts of concentrated mediocrity. Then this season of education will command the largest remuneration, as it will secure the finest powers to the work; and because such work cannot be pursued by any one person for many years, nor even for a short time without assistance, relieving from the ceaseless attention that a company of small children requires, for little children cannot be wound up to go like watches; but to keep them in order, the teacher must constantly meet their outbursting life with her own magnetic forces; while their employments must be continually interchanged, and mingled with their recreations.

Children ought to continue these Kindergarten exercises from the age of three to nine; and if faithfully taught, they could then go into what is called scholastic training, in a state of mind to receive from it the highest advantages it is capable of giving; free from the disadvantages which are now so obvious as to have raised, in our practical country, a party prejudiced against classical education altogether.

The preceding chapter and the one on Geometry, which succeeds, are rather for the direction of children in the last than the first years of the Kindergarten; for they go over into the second stage of education. Object-lessons, addressed more to the heart and imagination, grow directly out of the plays, as we have seen.

And, without any of the terms of Geometry, the sticklaying and the folding of paper give the child geometrical facts in a practical way; as well as counting, and all of arithmetic that precedes Colburn's "First Lessons," some of which can be taught even before teaching to read.

CHAPTER IX.

GEOMETRY.

Rev. Dr. Hill, the present President of Harvard College, in his articles in Dr. Barnard's "Journal of Education," has set forth the importance of Geometry in the earliest education, giving the Science of Form precedence to that of numbers. Of course he does not mean that logical demonstration is to form one of the exercises of little children! but that observation of differences and resemblances of shape, and the combination of forms, should be inwoven with the amusements of children. He invented a toy on the principle of the Chinese tanagram, (published by Hickling, Swan & Co., in Boston,) to further an exercise which begins in the cradle with the examination of the hands and feet.

The blocks are the first materials. Take the cube and ask how many faces it has; how many corners; and whether one face is larger than another or equal; and finally, lead the child to describe a cube as a solid figure with six equal sides, and eight corners. Then take a solid triangle from the box and draw out by questions that it has five sides and six corners, that three of its sides are equal, and two others equal; that the three larger sides are four-sided, and the two smaller sides are three-sided; and that the corners are sharper than those of a cube.

Make analogous use of all the blocks, and of the furniture of the room, of the sphere and its parts, the cylinder, &c. Do not require the definition-formulas at first, but content yourself with opening the children's eyes to the facts which the formula afterwards shall declare.

Paper-folding can be made subservient to another step, just short of abstraction.

Give each one of a class a square piece of paper, and proceed thus: What is the shape of this paper? How many sides has it? Which is the longest side? How many corners has it? Have in hand, already cut, several acute and obtuse angled triangles, and showing them, ask if the corners of the square are like these corners? If they are as sharp as some of them; or as blunt as some? Spreading out the triangle before them say, which is the sharpest corner, and which the bluntest? and let the children compare them with the corners of the square, by laying them upon the square. They will see that the square corners are neither blunt nor sharp, but as they will perhaps say, *straight*. Let them look round the room, and on the furniture and window-sashes, find these several kinds of corner. At least they can always find right angles in the furniture. Then tell them there is another word for corners, namely, *angles*, that a square corner is a *right* angle, a sharp corner a sharp angle, and a blunt corner a blunt angle.

If the teacher chooses she can go farther and tell them that *acute* is another word for sharp, and *obtuse* another word for blunt; (or these two *Latin words* may be deferred till by and by, one new word *angle* being enough to begin with.)

You can then say, "Now tell me how you describe a square, supposing somebody should ask you that did not know;" and give them more or less help to say: "A square is a figure with four equal sides and four straight corners (or right angles)." To prove to them that it is necessary to mention the right angles in describing a square, you can make a rhombus, and show them its different shape with its acute and obtuse angles. Having thus exhausted the description of a square, let every one double up his square, and so get an oblong. Ask if this is a square? What is it? How does it differ from a square? Are all four sides different from each other? Which sides are alike? How are the corners (or angles)? In what, then, is it like a square? In what does it differ? Bring out from the child at last the description of an oblong, as a four-sided figure with straight corners (or right angles), and its opposite sides equal. Contrast it with some parallelogram which is not a rectangle, and which you must have ready. Let them now fold their oblongs again, and crease the folds; then ask them to unfold and say what they have, and they will find four squares. Ask them if every square can be folded so as to make two oblongs, and then if every oblong can be so divided as to make two squares? If they say yes to this last question, give them a shorter oblong, which you must have ready, and having made them notice that it is an oblong, by asking them to tell whether its opposite sides are equal, and its angles right angles, ask them to fold it, and see if it will make two squares. They will see that it will not. Then ask them if all oblongs are of the same shape; and then if all squares are of the same shape?

The above foldings will be enough for a lesson, and if the children are small it will be enough for two lessons.

Beginning the next time, ask them what is the difference between an oblong and square? and if they have forgotten, do not tell them in words, but give them square papers and let them learn it over again as before, by their own observations. Then give them again square pieces of paper, and ask them to join the opposite corners, and crease a fold diagonally (but do not use the word diagonally). Then ask them what shape they have got? They will reply, a three-sided figure. Ask them how many corners or angles it has, and then tell them that, on account of its being three-cornered, it is called a *triangle*. Now let them compare the angles, and they will find that there is one straight corner (right angle) and two sharp corners (acute angles). Ask them if the sides are equal, and they will find that two sides are equal and the other side longer. Set up the triangle on its base, so that the equal sides may be in the attitude of the outstretched legs of a man; call their attention to this by a question, and then say, on account of this shape this triangle is called equal-legged, as well as right-angled—a right-angled equal-legged triangle. By giving them examples to compare it with, you can demonstrate to them that all right-angled triangles are not equal-legged, and all equal-legged triangles are not right-angled. Show them an equal-legged right-angled triangle, an equal-legged acute-angled triangle, and an equal-legged obtuse-angled triangle, and this discrimination will be obvious. The word *isosceles* can be introduced, if the teacher thinks best; but I keep off the Greek and Latin terms as long as possible.

Now tell the children to put together the other two corners of their triangles, laying the sharp corners on each other, and crossing the fold; unfolding their papers they will find four right-angled equal-legged triangles creased upon their square paper. Are all these of the same shape, and of the same size? Now fold the unfolded square into oblongs, and make a crease, and they will find, on unfolding again, that they have six isosceles triangles, two of them being twice as large as any one of the other four. Ask, are all these triangles of equal size? Are all of them similar in shape? leading them to discriminate the use in geometry of the words equal and similar. Can triangles be large and small without altering the shape? Then similar and equal mean differently? Are all squares similar? are all squares equal? are all triangles equal? are all triangles similar? What is the difference between a square and oblong? What is the difference between a square and a triangle? What is the difference between a square and a rhombus? What kind of corners has a rhombus? In what is a square like a rhombus? How do you describe a triangle? What is the name of the triangles you have learnt about? They will answer right-angled, equal-legged triangles. Then give them each a hexagon, and ask them what kind of corners it has? Whether any one is more blunt than another? Whether any side is greater than another? How many sides has it? And then draw out from them that a hexagon is a figure of six equal sides, with six obtuse angles, just equal to each other in their obtuseness. Having done this, direct the folding till they have divided the hexagon into six triangles, meeting at the centre. Ask them if these are right-angled triangles, and if they hesitate, give them a square to measure with. Then ask them if they are equal-legged (isosceles) triangles. They may say yes, in which case reply yes, and more than equal-legged, they are equal-*sided*. All three sides are equal, and so they have a different name,—they are called *equilateral*. Ask, what is the difference between equilateral and isosceles, if you have given them these names, and help them, if necessary, to the answer, "equilateral triangles have all the sides equal, isosceles triangles have only two sides equal." Are equilateral triangles all similar, that is, of the same shape? Are isosceles triangles all similar? and if they hesitate or say yes, show two isosceles triangles, one with the third side shorter, and one with it longer than the other two sides.

Now give to each child a square, and tell them to fold it so as to make two equal triangles; then to unfold it, and fold it into two equal oblongs. Unfold it again, and there will be seen, beside the triangles, two other figures, which are neither squares, oblongs, or triangles, but a four-sided figure of which no two sides are equal, and only two sides are parallel, with two right angles, one obtuse and one acute angle. Let all this be brought out of the children by questions. As there is no common name for this figure, name it trapezoid at once. Then let them fold the paper to make two parallelograms at right angles with the first two, and they will have two equal squares, and four equal isosceles triangles, which are equal to the two squares. Now fold the paper into two triangles, and you will have eight triangles meeting in the centre by their vertices, all of which are right-angled and equal-legged. Ask them if they are equal-sided? so as to keep them very clear of confounding the isosceles with the equilateral, but use the English terms as often as the Latin and Greek, for the vernacular keeps the mind awake, while the foreign *technical* puts it into a passiveness more or less sleepy. Then give all the children octagons, and bring out from them its description by sides and angles; and then fold it so as to make eight isosceles triangles.

Another thing that can be taught by paper-folding is to divide polygons, regular or irregular, into triangles, and thus let them learn that every polygon contains as many triangles as it has sides, less two.

Proportions can also be taught by letting them cut off triangles, similar in shape to the wholes, by creases parallel to the base. Grund's "Plane Geometry" will help a teacher to lessons on proportion, and can be almost wholly taught by this paper-folding. Also Professor Davies's "Descriptive Geometry," and Hay's "Symmetrical Drawing."

Of course it will take a teacher who is familiar with geometry to do all that may be done by this amusement, to habituate the mind to consider and compare forms, and their relations to each other. Exercises on folding circles can be added. It would take a volume to exhaust the subject. Enough has been said to give an idea to a capable teacher. Care must be taken that the consideration should be always of concrete not of abstract forms. Mr. Hill says his "First Lessons in Geometry" were the amusements of his son of five years old. Pascal and Professor Pierce found out such amusements for themselves, which had the high end of preparing them for their great attainments in logical geometry.

Sometimes surprising applications of Geometry, thus practically appreciated, will be made by very small people. A boy of eight years of age, with whom I read over Mr. Hill's "Geometry for Beginners" for his amusement, in two months after invented a self-moving carriage for his sister's dolly, that would give it a ride of ten feet! A neighboring carpenter made it from his drafted model.

CHAPTER X.

READING.

This art should be taught simultaneously with writing, or, more properly, printing; and I should certainly advise that it do not come till children are hard upon seven years old, if they have entered the Kindergarten at three. For it properly belongs to the second stage of education, after the Kindergarten exercises on the blocks, sticks, peas, &c., are entirely exhausted; and the children have become very expert in sewing, weaving, pricking, and drawing. They will then have received a certain cultivation of intellect which will make it possible to teach Reading on a philosophical method, which will make the acquisition a real cultivation of mind, instead of the distraction it now is to those whose vernacular is English, the *pot pourri* of languages, and whose *orthography* should be called *Kakography*, it is so lawless.

Though we repudiate phonography, so far as to deprecate its being applied to the English language, and reducing all our libraries to a dead language as it were, we are not insensible to the truth that *phonography* is the true principle of writing; and this method of ours takes advantage of it to a certain extent, as we shall proceed to show: for if we pronounce the vowel-characters as in the Italian language, and the letters c and g hard, it is a fact that the largest number of syllables in English will be found strictly phonographic. It was on this hint, given by a great philologist, that the "First Nursery Reading Book" was written, which has no word in it that makes an exception to the letters so sounded. In my own Kindergarten, where I began to teach reading when I was yet ignorant of the necessity for the previous training of which I have just given account, I began to teach on this method, reading and writing at the same time; thus:—

All the children were set before the black-board, with their slates and pencils; and I said, "What does the cat say?" The answer was immediately ready,—"mieaou." Now this sound goes from the highest to the lowest of the Italian vowels, beginning with the consonant m.

I said, "Now we will learn to print 'mieaou.' How does it begin?" I answered myself,—shutting my lips, and sounding m. They all imitated the sound, which, being a semi-vowel, was continuous.

I said, "We will write m," putting down three short perpendiculars, and joining them on top by a horizontal; and I made the letter myself, according to this direction, and they imitated with more or less success.

I then said, "*mi*," sounding the i as in mach*i*ne; and adding, "Now we must write i,—and that is one little short perpendicular with a dot over it." I did it, and they imitated.

Then I said "mie," sounding e as in egg, only making it long; "and this e is made by a curve and straight line,"—at the same time making it on the black-board, which they imitated.

Then I said "miea," sounding a as in ah; and, as I made it on the blackboard, I said, "We will make a little egg; and over the egg we will make a dot, and that is a snake's head; and this is the body," I continued, as I made the curve that completed the a. They imitated with indifferent success, but I did not criticise their scrawls.

Then I said, "miĕa*o*," and making the o, they imitated it easily.

Then I said, "miea*ou*," sounding the u not *yu*, but like u in Peru; and they imitated sound and character.

It proved quite an entertainment to repeat this lesson, till they were very expert. The next day I made them tell me the sounds, one by one, as I had done to them; and I wrote the letters. I also would write it, letter by letter; and they would sound first, m, then the syllable mi, then mie, then miea, then mieao, then mieaou. When they were perfectly familiar with these sounds and characters, I told them these letters were called vowels, or vocals, because they were the sounds of the voice.

In another lesson, I asked them how they made the sound m, and helped them to say that they did it by putting their lips together, and sounding without opening them; for I wanted the power of the character and not the name,—*em*; and then I said, "Now tell me how shall I write mama?" which they also wrote on their slates.

I then said that the lips made another motion when they began to say papa; that they were put together and opened without any sound of the voice at all,—at the same time showing it myself on my own lips. And I told them to write the letter p by making a straight perpendicular line, twice as long as the lines that made m; and then, at the upper right hand, drawing their upper lip,—also doing it myself for them to imitate. I then told them to put on an a after it, then another p, and then another a; and now they had papa.

I said, "You have now *articulated* with your lips two sounds, but you can make more articulations with your lips. You can put your lips just as you do to make p; and then, if you sound a little, you will make b; and when you write b, you can make a perpendicular line as you did to make p, but instead of putting an upper lip to it, put an under lip on the lower right-hand side of it;" and I showed how to do it on the black-board, and saw that they imitated it on the slate.

The next day I began with calling on them to write the vowels, dictating by the sounds I had given them; and then the lip letters, m, p, and b.

I then said, "But there are two more articulations with lips—Put your upper teeth on your lower lip and breathe" (articulating f at the same time). They imitated, and I said, "Now make a perpendicular line and cross it, and then make the top of the line bend over a little; that is the letter f" (I gave the power, not name, ef). "Now put your lip as before and breathe again, making a little sound, and instead of f it will be v. The letter v is printed by two short obliques meeting at the bottom. Now you can make all the lip letters, m, p, b, f, v."

For exercise in printing, and to make sure of these letters and sounds, I told them to write ma, pa, ba, fa, va, always keeping the Italian sounds of the vowel; also, me, pe, be, fe, ve; mi, pi, bi, fi, vi; mo, po, bo, fo, vo; and mu, pu, bu, fu, vu.

Another lesson was the tooth letters d, t, s. Here the teeth must be set together, and a sound made for d; and the lip put behind the perpendicular in printing it; the teeth put together, the articulation t is made without putting any voice to it. The teeth put together, and a hissing sound makes s. The letter can be described as a snake, the head on the right and the tail on the left of the curl: z is still more easily made by three lines.

These letters can be made fast in the memory, by dictating di, de, da, do, du; ti, te, ta, to, tu; si, se, sa, so, su; and zi, ze, za, zo, zu.

Then attention is drawn to throat letters. The easiest to make is h. Let them see that the sound is breathed out of their throats, and do not give it the name of *aitch*. They can write ha, hi, he, ho, and hu; and then make the sound k, and show them how it is written: sometimes k, sometimes q, and sometimes c; and do not call c *see*. Make them write ca, co, cu; ka, ke, ki, ko, ku; and qua, que, qui, quo.

Show them how to write the sonorous throat letter in go, ga, gu. It will be very easy for them to make the nose sound n, and write the letter by two short perpendiculars, joined on top by a horizontal line; the tongue sound l and the rolling r are also easily sounded and written. In a week's lessons, or possibly a fortnight's, these letters can all be learned; but it is of no consequence if it takes a month.

Another way of learning the letters is given on a subsequent page (the 79th); but this has the advantage of being a little more scientific, and exercising the classifying instinct, which has been considerably developed by the exercises involved in the occupations.

On account of the irregularity of what is called English orthoepy and orthography, the written language is a chaos—into which, when the child's mind is introduced in the usual way, all its natural attempts at classification are baffled. The late Horace Mann, in a lecture on the alphabet, has with great humor and perspicacity shown this; and he recommended that children should be taught to read by *words* purely. But when some years afterwards his attention was drawn to the phonic method, he accepted it fully; and wrote for Mrs. Mann the preface to her Philadelphia edition of the Primer of Reading and Drawing. This was not until after it had been tested in his own family and some others, where I had introduced the phonic method.

On the details of my method I must enlarge all the more, because I find myself differing in some respects from Mr. Sheldon's plan, which loses a large part of the advantages of the phonic method by not having one definite sound for each letter. As I have taught on my plan successfully for fifteen years, I am prepared to defend it at all points, from the ground of a various experience. But I can adduce also the highest philologic authority for my mode of sounding the alphabet,[E] as well as an argument of common sense from the nature of the case.

The primal cause of the chaotic condition of English orthography, is the fact that the Roman alphabet, which was a perfect phonography of the old Latin language, lacked characters for four English vowels and four English consonants. The Latin monks had not the wit to invent new characters for these additional sounds; but undertook to use the Roman letters for them also. Hence for the vowel heard in the words irk, err, work, and urge, they used indifferently all four characters; for truly one would do as well as another. But if they had put a dot into the middle of the o, and added it to the alphabet, it would have been better than either. Also, if for the vowel sound of pun, they had put a dot under the u; and for the vowel sound of man, they had put a dot under the a; and for the vowel sound of not, a dot under the o; they would have had four more letters in their alphabet, which would have completed the phonography of the English vowels. Similar dots under d t s c would have made a phonography of consonants, and avoided the awkward combinations of sh, ch, and the ambiguity of th, which now stands for the differing initials of *then* and *thin*.

But as they did not do this, a certain divorce took place between the ideas of the sounds and the letters; and hence the long uncertainty of the English orthography, and the stereotyped absurdities which now mark it.

It is so nearly impossible to remedy a difficulty which has passed into print so largely, that we have to accept the evil, and remedy as best we may the disadvantage it is to young minds to have all this confusion presented to them on the threshold of their literary education.[F]

It was suggested to me by Dr. Kraitsir, that I should take a volume of any book, and count the times that each of the vowels, and c and g, were sounded as the Romans sounded them, and how many times they were sounded otherwise, and thus see whether it was true, as he said, that these Roman sounds were the most frequent, even in the English language. I did so on a few pages of Sir Walter Scott's novels, and found that the letter i sounded as in *ink* 240 times, to one that it sounded as in *bind*; and though the proportion was not quite so great with any other vowel, yet there was a large majority for the Roman sound, in each instance, as well as for the hard sounds of c and g. Indeed I found g was hard, even before e and i, in the case of every Saxon word; and that all the soft gs, which are not many, were derived from the Norman-French.

I then set myself to find what words in English were written entirely with the Roman-sounding letters; and, to my surprise, found a large number,—enough to fill a primary spelling-book;—while most of the syllables of the rest of the words in the language yielded on analysis the same sounds. It immediately occurred to me to begin to teach children to read by these words, whose analysis would always yield them the Roman sounds, and reserve, till afterwards, the words which are exceptions, leaving the anomalies to be learnt by rote.

I tried my first experiment on a child a little more than four years old, by printing on a black-board certain words, letter by letter, until he had learned the whole alphabet, both to know each character at sight, and to print it on the black-board, and it was a signal success.

For the convenience of those who do not know the old Roman pronunciation of Latin, for which our alphabet is a perfect phonography, I will give the sounds of the letters here.

In the case of the vowels (*voice letters*),

i	is pronounced	ĭh as in ink,	(not eye.)
e	"	ĕh as in ell,	(not as in be.)
a	"	ăh as in arm,	(not as in may.)
o	"	ŏh as in old,	
u	"	ŭh as in ruin,	(not as in unit.)

in the case of the consonants, giving the power of the letter by making them finals, and obscuring the e as much as possible for the lip letters, ĕb, ĕf, ĕp, ĕv, while the semi-vowels m, n, l, r, require not even the obscure ĕ to their being sounded perfectly, shutting the lips and sounding m, opening them and shutting the palate to sound n, holding the tongue still to sound l, shaking it to sound r, (ĕl, ĕm, ĕn, ĕr;) the tooth letters ĕd, ĕt, ĕss, ĕzz—and the throat letters ĕc, ĕk, eq,[G] eg, and a breathing from the throat for h. Often children will come to the Kindergarten knowing the letters, in which case it is best to begin with the letters according to the organs, as is suggested in my first chapter, and when they give the old names—you can say, "No, I do not want that name but the sound."

The whole alphabet in order will then be ăh, ĕb, ĕc, ĕd, ĕh, ĕf, ĕg, h (breathed), ĭh, ĕj, ĕk, ĕl, ĕm, ĕn, ŏh, ĕp, ĕq, ĕr, ĕss, ĕt, ŭh (oo) ĕv, w (breathed) ĕx, y, just like ĭh, and not called wye, ĕz. Also the sign & for the word *and*.

In the first part of this chapter, I have detailed one method of beginning with a class,—that of giving the sounds of the letters first, classed according to the organs.

But my common way is to begin with whole words, which are more sure to interest a child. A limited number of words arranged in sentences, teaches them to know and write the whole alphabet. For the convenience of teachers who may not have either my "First Nursery Reading-Book," or Mrs. Mann's "Primer of Reading and Drawing" on hand, I will give here some sentences that contain the whole alphabet, which the teacher can teach by printing them on the black-board, and letting the children imitate them with pencil on the slate, or chalk on the black-board.

O puss, puss, pussy; O kitty, kitty, kitty; Kitty sings miu, miu; pussy sings mieaou; pussy is old, pussy is cold; put pussy into mamma's basket;

mamma is singing to papa; papa is kissing mamma; pussy, go to kitty, go, go, go; kitty is in mamma's basket; go into mamma's garden, and pick roses, anemones, tulips, and pinks; mamma's velvet dress fits well; bells ring and cars go; cars go very quickly; hens sit; hens eggs; eggs in lark's nest; eggs in linnet's nest; larks sing tralala, tralala; fill mamma's basket full of roses, anemones, pinks, tulips, crocuses; Lizzy is dizzy, very dizzy; Helen is rosy red; Alexis sent his mamma a jar full of jelly; Barbara kisses Cora; Dora is spinning yarn; Flora is spinning yarn; Gilbert sent Henry a jar of guava jelly; Isabella is kissing Julia; Karlito sent a linnet's egg to Lilian; Margaret picks roses; Nina picks tulips in Olivia's garden; Penelope plants pinks in Ellen's garden; Rosalind sings to Quasi-modo; Susan puts eggs into mamma's basket; Tina brings roses to Vivian; Willy brings crocuses to mamma.

The above sentences, written over and over again, will teach all the letters; others must be added, but after certain letters are learnt, it is useful, and a pleasant variety, for the children to write columns of words, with only one letter differing; thus, old, cold, fold, gold, hold, sold, told, wold; ell, bell, dell, fell, hell, quell, sell, tell, well; art, cart, dart, hart, mart, part, tart, start; in, binn, din, fin, jin, kin, pin, sin, tin, win, &c., &c.

My "First Nursery Reading-Book" is entirely made up of such columns, after half a dozen pages of words in sentences; and long before the children have written it half through, they can pronounce the words on first sight, though many of them are five and six syllables long.

And here I must foreclose some criticisms which have been made on this book.

First,—that the sentences are not interesting or important. That is of no moment. Children are interested in separate words; especially if they are to write them as well as read them. I have never seen children tired of the words, and of making them.

Some persons have disputed the pronunciation of some of the words. There are, perhaps, half a dozen inadvertencies in the book which can be corrected in a second edition.

I indicate no difference between the s when it is sounded sharp, and when soft like z. But I think this will never lead to any practical error; because the language is vernacular, and the child has a teacher.

I affirm that the article *a* is sounded ah in the *spoken* language, when it is not accented. Also that in such words as deject, reject, &c., the two e's sound alike, like most unaccented e's in the language.

For a time, there is no need for the children to have a book at all. Let them have a lesson fifteen minutes long in which they write the words after the dictation of the teacher.

Let the written words remain on the black-board, and after some other employments have intervened, let them read the words off the black-board.

When they have mastered all the letters, it is a good plan to give them the book, and let them find the words. Showing them a line, ask them to look along and find a certain word.

They will be pleased to find that they can read in a book, and will like to copy on their slates the columns of words, which may be made another exercise of a quarter of an hour. In my Kindergarten, they write the words, after the teacher, on their blackboards; and afterwards write out of the printed books upon the slate. I have hitherto had more time, in proportion, given to the reading than my own judgment quite approves; because parents are so urgent, and measure their children's progress so exclusively by their power of reading; and, if they do not learn a great deal faster than children usually learn to read, distrust the system, and interfere.

Even if this method did prove longer than other methods of learning to read, I should wish to pursue it, because to find that the same letter always represents the same sound, cultivates the mind's power of classification, and gives it confidence in its own little reasoning. But I have found that it is a shorter, not a longer, process. I have known a child of three years old, who was found to know how to read, when there was no thought of teaching him, but his brother of five years old had been taught to read upon the black-board in his presence. A child of seven years old learnt to read and write print beautifully, in three months, in lessons of ten minutes, given only when she asked for them. And in those cases there was not the additional advantage of a class. Several children in my own Kindergarten, in my first season, when I never gave half an hour in the day to reading, not only mastered my first Nursery Reading-Book, but got upon the anomalous words, and learnt to read so far, that the second season they could read fluently. If as much time was given, in the Kindergarten, to mere reading, as is given in the public schools, they would, doubtless, have learnt in three months, but I would not give the time; for I believe it is so much better for the whole nature, *i. e.*, all the powers of sense and apprehension, to be cultivated by examining objects.

I have also another difficulty to contend with. Children are taught their letters at home, and the parents interfere to help, and really hinder by bringing in the old sounds of the letters and the anomalous words, before I am ready for them. There is no objection to the children's having the First Nursery-Book at home to use and copy on their slates, provided those at home will confine themselves to pronouncing the words to them instead of attempting to spell them.

The question, however, comes at last, But how are they to attain the rest of the language? Before I had any experience, I myself thought this was to be a great difficulty. In the first instance, after I had brought my little pupil to the point that he could print correctly any word that I pronounced to him, and could read at sight any of my selected words, I gave him a piece of poetry to read, beginning—

"Sleep, baby, sleep."

He read it *slay-ape bahby, slay-ape*.

I said, "No, that first word is *sleep*." He was surprised, and wondered why it was written so.

I said, "Perhaps they used to say *slayape*, but they say *sleep* now; and in books there are a good many such words. Now I will rub out sl (I pronounced this combination with one impulse of the voice) and put a *w*, and say, now, what is that?" "O, That is *weep*." Now I rubbed out the *w*, and put *d*. He immediately said, "That is deep." I said, "Now you write sleep, and under it put weep, deep, peep, keep, steep, sweep, creep." He did so, at once, and then he took great pleasure in getting a paper and lead-pencil, and writing the whole column, which, of course, he never forgot. I proceeded in the same manner, till he had not only written all the song, but all the analogues of each word,—and it was wonderful how soon he could read. The scientific habit of mind which was attained by classing the words as he learned them, has shown itself throughout his education. He never learned a so-called spelling-lesson, but he scarcely ever wrote a word wrongly spelled; and it has been a uniform observation that children taught on this method always write without errors. Each variation from the standard so strongly fixed in their minds makes a great impression; and to write the words in groups, makes these anomalies remembered in groups.

In my own Kindergarten, I give to my class "Mother Goose's Melodies." They know many of them by heart; but I make them sit in class, and each, in turn, read one word, in order to teach them to keep the place, and when they finish a verse, I ask them to find some word, and often make it the nucleus of a group of words of the same kind, to be written upon the blackboard and slates as above. But I think it is a good plan, before giving a book, to call their attention to the initial sounds of *thin, then, shin, chin*, and ask them what letter stands for these. Of course they will say they do not know. Then you can say "There is none; for the people who made these letters did not have these sounds in their language; and so, when they came to write English, they put a *t* and *h* together to stand for one sound; and *c* and *h* for another; and *s* and *h* for another."

Lists of words should then be dictated and written: such as thin, think, thing, thrift, thrill, thick, bath, lath, doth, sloth, quoth, pith, smith, fifth, filth, width, depth, tenth, truth, thresh, threshold, methodist, synthetic, pathetic, cathartic, then, them, with, this, hither, thither, nether, tether, hitherto, farthing, withhold, brethren, char, chart, charm, chaff, chant, larch, march, parch, starch, chest, chess, chin, chick, chill, chit, chink, chintz, rich, chirrup, inch, pinch, clinch, flinch, winch, finch, filch, milch, clinch, trench, bench, wrench, quench, shin, ship, sharp, shark, shed, shell, shelf, shaft, shorn, shred, shrift, shrimp, shrill, flesh, mesh, fresh, dish, fish, wish, harsh, marsh, sheriff, shiver, relish, cherish, perish, freshet, finish, prudish, bluish, garnish, tarnish, varnish, blemish, refresh. Attention can then be called to the words beginning with *wh*, which are pronounced (as they were *written* in Saxon) by uttering the *h* before the *w*; as when, whet, whelk, whelp, whelm, wherry, whiz, whig, whip, whiff, whist, whisk, whirl, which, whimper, pronounced hwen, hwet, &c.

I suppose I need not say that the consideration of one of the extra consonants will be enough for one lesson.

The next step is to learn the diphthongs, that is, the proper—which I consider the only—diphthongs. Make the children pronounce oi, and see that two sounds are slid together; and then let them write on their slates, in different columns, boil, coil, foil, soil, toil, moil, spoil, coin, join, groin, point, joint, joist, hoist, foist, moist, cloister, surloin, exploit, void, &c.; also boy, coy, joy, toy, cloy, loyal, royal, envoy, enjoy, &c.

Then let them pronounce the diphthong *ou*, and write in one column the words out, our, thou, loud, proud, cloud, noun, bound, found, hound, mound, pound, round, sound, wound, bout, clout, flout, lout, gout, pout, rout, sprout, spout, shout, snout, stout, mouth, south, couch, crouch, slouch, pouch, vouch, roundabout, bounty, county, amount, abound, scoundrel, discount, expound, about, &c.; and in another, how, cow, bow, mow, now, vow, owl, scowl, brow, prow, howl, gown, brown, crown, drown, cowl, fowl, crowd, clown, frown, vowel, towel, trowel, prowess. Call attention to the proper diphthong, which we write with what we call i long, (but it is no sound of ĭh at all,) and which the Romans wrote as a diphthong with two letters, ae and ai, pronouncing it as we do the i in ire. Then let them write in columns bind, find, grind, hind, blind, kind, mind, rind, wind, violet, dialect, inquiry, horizon, &c.

This same diphthong is also written with the Greek y,—in my, thy, cry, try, fry, wry, fly, ply, asylum, dynasty, petrify, signify, vilify, vivify, simplify, rectify, edify, notify, &c.

Call attention lastly, to the diphthong yu, written first with the letter u simply, as in unit, humid, fuel, cubic, stupid, putrid, mutual, funeral, singular, bitumen, acumen, nutriment; and secondly with ew, as few, chew, pew, new, mew, mewl, eschew, sinew; thirdly with iew, as view; fourthly with eu, as in eulogy, European, &c.; sometimes with eau, as in beauty and its compounds.

There is no propriety in calling *au* a diphthong, as it is one sound, and not two sounds. It is one of the extra vowels of the English language, written when short with o (though it is no sound of o proper) a, aw, and oa.

And now we come to the consideration of the extra vowels, beginning with this sound heard short in *not*, and long in the name of a carpenter's tool, awl.

Explain that there is no character for this vowel in the Roman alphabet, because the sound was not in the Latin language, and then proceed to show how it is written in various ways: first with an o, as in bob, cob, fob, gob, job, mob, nob, rob, sob, cock, dock, hock, lock, clock, flock, mock, pock, frock, rock, crock, shock, sock, cod, hod, nod, pod, odd, shod, rod, sod, trod, doff, off, of, (pronounced ov,) cog, dog, fog, hog, jog, log, nog, doll, loll, poll, on, don, ton, pond, fond, blond, won, fop, drop, crop, lop, mop, pop, sop, top, chop, shop, stop, swop, prop, ox, box, fox, pox, moth, loth, froth, broth, lot, cot, dot, got, hot, jot, not, pot, rot, sot, tot, wot, grot, clot, shot, spot, boss, cross, dross, floss, loss, moss, toss, gloss, cost, frost, lost, tost, bond, fond, pond, pomp, romp. Then show that it is written sometimes with an a, as in all, fall, call, hall, gall, tall, wall, small, stall, ball, thrall, squall, squash, squad, squat, quart, war, dwarf, scald, bald, salt, halt, swab, ward, sward, warn, warp, warm, wand, want, was, wast, wash, swan, watch, swamp, waltz, wasp; sometimes with *au*, as in daub, fraud, gaudy, fault, vault, paunch, craunch, laurel, haul, caul, maul, augury, autumnal; and sometimes with *aw*, as in caw, daw, draw, haw, hawk, jaw, law, maw, paw, claw, straw, raw, thaw, squaw, saw, flaw, awl, shawl, bawl, brawn, drawn, awning, tawny, awkward, tawdry, sawyer, mawkish, lawful; also with oa in broad.

Another extra vowel, heard in the word man, is written, in default of a character for it, with a, as in cab, dab, gab, jab, nab, hack, back, jack, lack, pack, rack, crack, clack, black, bad, gad, glad, had, lad, mad, pad, sad, shad, bag, cag, fag, gag, hag, lag, nag, rag, crag, shag, sag, tag, wag, mall, shall, am, dam, flam, ham, sham, jam, an, ban, can, fan, clan, man, pan, ran, band, hand, land, stand, strand, grand, brand, cap, flap, gap, chap, lap, clap, map, nap, pap, sap, tap, at, bat, cat, fat, gat, hat, that, mat, pat, rat, brat, sat, spat, sprat, tat, vat. This same vowel is heard in the word plaid.

A third extra vowel is heard in *pun*, and written generally with an u; as cub, dub, hub, nub, rub, scrub, drub, tub, buck, duck, luck, cluck, muck, pluck, suck, stuck, truck, tuck, chuck, bud, cud, dud, mud, suds, stud, scud, buff, cuff, luff, bluff, muff, puff, stuff, ruff, scuff, bug, dug, drug, hug, jug, lug, slug, shrug, mug, snug, tug, cull, dull, gull, hull, mull, null, scull, gum, hum, drum, glum, plum, mum, rum, sum, bun, dun, gun, pun, run, sun, tun, stun, shun, up, cup, sup, bump, crump, dumps, gump, hump, jump, lump, mumps, pump, rump, us, buss, fuss, muss, rush, crush, gush, hush, mush, tush, bust, dust, gust, just, lust, must, rust, crust, but, cut, gut, hut, jut, nut, rut, tut, bunk, funk, sunk, drunk, trunk, hunt, punt, blunt, grunt, brunt, lunch, bunch, hunch, munch, punch, bulk, sulk, skulk, gulp, pulp, gulf, tuft, bung, hung, lung, clung, rung, stung, swung, strung, musk, rusk, dusk, tusk, busk, mulct, buskin, musket, runlet, bucket, public. This same sound is written with o in mother, brother, some, come, &c., and ou in touch, and in rough, tough, enough, in which *gh* sounds like ff.

The fourth extra vowel in English having no character for it is written, first, with i, as irk, shirk, dirk, kirk, mirk, quirk, bird, gird, whirl, quirl, girl, firm, first, chirp, shirt, sir, fir, stir, flirt, spirt, squirt, squirm, girdle, &c. Secondly, with e, as in err, her, herd, term, fern, pert, wert, overt, clerk, sperm, stern, insert, vermin, perhaps, perplex, persist, expert, divert, superb, sterling, verdict, pervert, ferment, fervent, servant, perfect, serpent, partner, sever, several, inter, internal, fraternal, paternal, maternal, external, infernal, interdict, intermix, infer; and generally the final er, as silver, toper, &c. Thirdly, this vowel is written with o, as in work, worm, word, worst, world, worth; and the final or, as in arbor, ardor, vigor, &c. Fourthly, with an *u*, as in urn, burn, turn, churn, spurn, cur, fur, blur, bur, purr, spur, curb, suburb, surd, curd, surf, scurf, turf, turk, lurk, curl, furl, hurl, hurdle; and the finals ur, or, and ture, as arbor, honor, perjure, injure, &c.

Another anomaly of English orthography is the silent e, at the end of so many words; as doe, foe, hoe, roe, toe, cue, clue, blue, glue, flue, give, live, lucre, axle, noble, ogle, reptile, fertile, sterile, sextile, flexible, futile, missile, famine, jasmine, destine, pristine, frigate, senate, reptile, legate, pensive, missive, active, captive, festive, motive, sportive, illusive, defective, objective, elective, invective, perspective, defensive, expensive, preventive, retentive, progressive, vindictive, restrictive, instinctive, descriptive, explosive, corrosive, delusive, exclusive, inclusive, preclusive, intensive, palliative, narrative, relative, privative, lucrative, intuitive, infinitive, explicative, figurative, imitative, indicative, superlative, diminutive, retrospective, barnacle, spectacle, miracle, pinnacle, article, particle, ventricle, edible, credible, flexible, audible, enoble, ignoble, sensible, senile, juvenile, feminine, eglantine, multiple, dissemble, assemble, quadrille, clandestine, intestine, determine, illumine, calibre, ferule, marble, pebble, treble, tremble, nibble, quibble, scribble, nimble, meddle, peddle, kindle, spindle, fiddle, riddle, griddle, quiddle, middle, twinkle, gargle, single, mingle, sparkle, speckle, sickle, tickle, trickle, dimple, simple, pimple, ripple, triple, pickle, grizzle, little, brittle, spittle, whittle, nettle, settle, kettle, startle, tinkle, sprinkle, valise, marine, ravine, machine, Alexandrine, creditable, and other words having the final syllable *ble*.

This silent e final is found also in words which have the diphthong i; as bide, glide, hide, chide, ride, side, slide, tide, wide, bride, fife, life, wife, rife, strife, bribe, jibe, dike, like, bile, file, mile, pile, tile, vile, wile, smile, while, style, dime, time, mime, chime, rime, prime, crime, dine, fine, thine, line, nine, mine, pine, spine, shine, wine, swine, twine, vine, kine, chine, pipe, wipe, ripe, gripe, snipe, tripe, stripe, type, vie, dire, fire, hire, mire, shire, sire, tire, lyre, wire, spire, squire, tribe, scribe, bribe, jibe, bite, kite, mite, smite, kite, write, white, trite, wise, lithe, blithe, writhe, strive, thrive, drive, wive, alive, size, prize, agonize, paralyze, sympathize, symbolize, &c.

E may also be considered silent, it is so obscure, in many words ending in el and en; as harden, bidden, golden, garden, sicken, quicken, thicken, stricken, broken, spoken, token, swollen, stolen, open, kitten, mitten, smitten, bitten, given, molten, driven, woven, frozen, mizzen, dizzen, tinsel, morsel, swivel, drivel, novel, model, level, bevel, eleven, seven, &c.

U and e are both silent in the words rogue, brogue, fugue, eclogue, prologue, apologue, epilogue, intrigue, fatigue, synagogue, demagogue, pedagogue, decalogue, catalogue, mystagogue, picturesque, burlesque, grotesque, pique, casique.

U is silent in guess, guest, guard, gaunt, flaunt, taunt, daunt, avaunt, launch, staunch, laundry, laundress, liquor, piquet, coquette, paroquet, exchequer, palanquin, guarantee, gauntlet, saunter, guilt, guitar, built, build, biscuit, four, pour, court, gourd, mould, bourn, soul, moult, shoulder, poultry, coulter; and w final, when preceded by vowels, except when ow stands for ou diphthong, is silent.

I is silent in fruit, suit, recruit, bruise, cruise, heifer, surfeit, forfeit, counterfeit, Madeira, and y in they, prey, whey, obey, heyday, convey, survey, purvey.

W is silent in bow, low, mow, row, sow, tow, slow, blow, glow, flow, snow, row, crow, grow, throw, bowl, own, blown, flown, grown, sown, mown, growth, owner, toward, below, lower, disown, arrow, barrow, farrow, harrow, marrow, fallow, gallows, hallow, shallow, sallow, tallow, bellow, fellow, yellow, shadow, burrow, furrow, billow, pillow, willow, widow, minnow, winnow, follow, hollow, morrow, sorrow.

A is silent in boat, coat, goat, doat, moat, groat, bloat, throat, loath, oath, boast, coast, roast, coax, hoax, oak, soak, cloak, coach, poach, roach, broach, goad, load, coal, foal, goal, shoal, oaf, loaf, foam, loam, roam, loan, moan, groan, soap, oar, boar, soar, board, hoard, hoarse, hoary, cocoa, gloaming, encroach, reproach, approach.

The silent consonants are k before n—(doubtless pronounced in Saxon times,) in knit, knee, knell, kneel, knave, knife, knack, know, knead, knives, knock, knuckle.

Also, g before n, as gnat, gnaw, gnarl, gnome, gnash, reign, deign, sign, consign, assign, design, condign, benign, impugn, oppugn, arraign, campaign.

Also, g before m, as phlegm, paradigm, &c.

Also, ch in schism and drachm.

Also, l before m, k, v, f, and d—as in alms, balm, calm, qualm, calf, half, talk, balk, stalk, chalk, walk, folks, salve, halves, calves, could, would, should, almond, salmon.

Also, p before s, and sh, as in pshaw, pseudo, psalm, psalter.

Also, b before t, as debt, doubt, subtle, indebted, undoubted, &c.

And b after m is silent, as lamb, jamb, climb, tomb, womb, numb, thumb, crumb, dumb, plumb, comb, hecatomb, catacomb, currycomb, coxcomb, succumb.

Also, n after m, as column, solemn, autumn, condemn, hymn, &c.

And d before t in stadtholder.

K is often unnecessarily used after c, and t before ch.

T after s is silent in listen, glisten, hasten, chasten, christen, fasten, moisten, thistle, whistle, bristle, castle, nestle, pestle, gristle, jostle, justle, hustle, bustle, rustle, epistle, apostle, mistletoe, forecastle.

C after s is silent in scion, scent, scythe, muscle, sceptre, science, sciatica, sciolism, scissure, scission, scissors, scenery, transcend, descend, descent, viscid, crescent, proboscis, fascinate, viscera, ascetic, excrescence, corpuscle, acquiesce, coalesce, rescission, abscission, putrescence, ascendency, susceptible, irascible, viscidity, eviscerate, lascivious, resuscitate, scimitar, scintillate, phosphoresce, deliquesce, effloresce, effervesce, transcendent, condescend, condescension, convalescence, concupiscence, reminiscence, acquiescent, iridescent, arborescent, susceptibility, scenography, sciography.

The initial h is often silent, as in hour, herbage, huge, honest, honor, humor; also, after r, rhomboid, rheum, rhyme, myrrh, ghost, aghast, catarrh, rhubarb, catarrhal, rheumatic, dishabille, rhapsody, posthumous, hemorrhage, &c.

W is silent before r in wry, write, writhe, wrath, wreath, wreathe, wrong, wretch, wright, wrist, wriggle, wrinkle; and before h in who, whose, whom, whoop, whole.

What is especially puzzling about the English orthography, is the unnecessary use of the same letter for different sounds. Thus s does not always sound s—but sometimes sounds like z. (If all the sounds z were written z, it would make our language look as full of z's as the Polish.)

After all the sonorous labials, gutturals, and dentals, we cannot help sounding z—as cabs, hods, rags, etc.; also, before m, as heroism, paroxysm, somnambulism, materialism, &c.; in monosyllables ending with a single s, as is, was, as, has, his, hers, ours, theirs; also, in daisy, reside, desire, noisy, bosom, visage, closet, resign, music, prison, reason, pansy, tansy, disown, preside, pleasant, peasant, prosaic, present, presence, Tuesday, measles, cosmos, pleasure, measure, treasure, leisure, disclosure, enclosure, composure, kerseymere, resolute, devisor, revisal, reprisal, basilisk, deposit, courtesan, raspberry, residue, venison, disaster, division, plausible, feasible, basilicon, presbytery, resolute, deposit, president, visionary, perquisite, exquisite, composite, resentment, carousal, espousal, disposal.

Instead of c or k we have in many words ch—as Christ, chasm, chyle, conch, chrome, ache, scheme, school, chaos, epoch, chorus, chronic, echo, anchor, tetrarch, trochee, archives, scholar, schooner, monarch, hierarch, chronicle, chrysalis, technical, mechanic, patriarch, pentateuch, bacchanal, saccharine, chamomile, eucharist, character, archetype, orchestra, catechize, catechism, alchemy, chemistry, schedule, paschal, chaldee, stomach, lilach, sumach, chimera, heptarchy, lachrymal.

All the above words are from the Greek, and so are those in which f is written with ph, as sylph, lymph, sphere, sphinx, graphic, phalanx, phantom, orphan, dolphin, camphor, pamphlet, sulphur, zephyr, hyphen, trophy, philter, phaeton, spheroid, alphabet, emphasis, prophesy, prophecy, caliphate, sophistry, &c.

The sound of s is substituted for the Latin guttural (hard c) in acid, placid, facile, tacit, process, precinct, docile, recipe, illicit, cinder, fleecy, census, pencil, precept, accede, recede, concede, cite, pacify, lacerate, macerate, taciturn, oscillate, precede, implicit, explicit, decimal, precipice, specify, specimen, abbacy, imbecile, indocile, solicit, felicity, atrocity, ferocity, rapacity, tenacity, veracity, vivacity, voracity, audacity, precocity, simplicity, lubricity, rusticity, municipal, medicinal, rhinoceros, publicity, diocesan, mendacity, mendicity, duplicity, elasticity, pertinacity, incapacity, electricity, multiplicity, authenticity, duodecimo, anticipates, necessary, countenance, abstinence, and all other words which end in ce.[H]

The sound of j is substituted for that of g (the sonorous guttural) in germ, genus, genius, angel, gentile, pigeon, dungeon, surgeon, sturgeon, bludgeon, curmudgeon, sergeant, pageant, vengeance, stingy, dingy, &c.,

manger, danger, stranger, religion, badger, budget, gibbet, giblets, allegiance, plagiarism, gibe, (sometimes and better jibe;) all words ending in ge, as bilge, huge, barge, large, and all ending in dge, as wedge, ledge, pledge, hedge, sledge, fledge, ridge, bridge, midge, drudge, judge, lodge; all words ending gious, as prodigious, egregious, sacrilegious, &c.; or in geous, as courageous, &c.; or in age, as cottage, plumage, foliage, &c.

The extra consonant which we sometimes write sh, is written variously; 1st, simply with s, as in sugar, sensual, and sure, and its compounds; 2dly, with ss, in cassia; 3dly, with ci, in magician, logician, patrician, optician, musician, academician, geometrician, mathematician; and in a multitude of words ending in ious, as specious, gracious, spacious, avaricious, auspicious, pertinacious, judicious, suspicious, loquacious, audacious, sagacious, fallacious, capacious, rapacious, tenacious, delicious, malicious, pertinacious, officious, capricious, ferocious, atrocious, precocious, voracious, veracious, and perhaps some others; also, in words ending with al, as official, judicial, provincial, commercial, artificial, beneficial; and in sociable, associate, appreciable and appreciate, enunciate, dissociate, excruciate, depreciate, emaciate, denunciate, renunciate, prescient, omniscient; 4thly, with ce, in cetaceous, filaceous, herbaceous, caduceous, cretaceous, testaceous, crustaceous, argillaceous, gallinaceous; 5thly, with ti, in factious, fractious, captious, vexatious, facetious, licentious, factitious, propitious, flagitious, nutritious, expeditious, superstitious, adventitious; vitiate, expatiate, ingratiate, insatiate, initiate; partial, martial, nuptial, initial, essential, substantial, credential, potential, prudential, solstitial, impartial, penitential, equinoctial, influential, reverential, pestilential, providential, circumstantial, ratio, and all words ending in tion, as ration, nation, station, notion, diction, fiction, friction, fraction, potion, action, junction, suction, section, mention, libation, vacation, vocation, location, exhalation, installation, implication, flagellation, appellation, revelation, education, &c.; 6thly, with ch, as chicanery, seneschal.

In many words is a superfluous t, as in hitch, ditch, pitch, witch, switch, stitch, flitch, stretch, sketch, etch, fetch, wretch, notch, botch, hotch, potch, watch, latch, match, batch, catch, hatch, patch, hutch.

In some words is a superfluous d, as badge, ledge, sledge.

And a superfluous k is very common.

Some of the above substitutions are perhaps natural enough, in consequence of the fact of extra sounds, having no special characters for them in the alphabet, which was phonography for the Latin language only. But there are the same perplexing changes with respect to the regular vowels.

Thus, in the case of e, when it is long, as in fête,—we find it written in five ways,—ay, ai, ea, ey, and simply a.

As 1st, aye, day, bay, fay, gay, hay, pay, may, nay, say, ray, dray, bray, gray, fray, play, pray, array, assay, allay, display, portray, dismay, mislay.

2d. Aid, braid, laid, maid, paid, afraid, staid, bait, gait, wait, bail, fail, hail, jail, mail, nail, pail, quail, rail, sail, tail, wail, frail, flail, snail, trail, avail, entail, assail, fain, gain, lain, main, pain, rain, vain, wain, train, grain, brain, stain, sprain, swain, drain, dainty, portrait, saint, faint, paint, quaint, plaint, aim, claim, maim, tailor, jailer, traitor, sailor, raiment, caitiff, plaintiff, prevail, contain, chilblain, sustain, upbraid, declaim, exclaim, proclaim.

3d. Break, steak, great.

4thly. They, convey, survey, &c.

5thly. Any, many, legation, asparagus, virago, volcano, verbatim, arcanum, potato, octavo, tornado, and words ending in ace, ade, afe, age, ake, ale, ame, ane, ape, ase, ate, athe, ave, ary, aste, aze, base, case, face, grace, lace, mace, pace, ace, bade, fade, shade, made, wade, safe, chafe, cage, sage, rage, gage, stage, page, wage, plumage, foliage, cottage, bake, cake, lake, make, quake, rake, take, sake, brake, flake, bale, dale, gale, hale, male, pale, sale, tale, whale, vale, bane, cane, fane, lane, mane, pane, sane, wane, vane, bathe, lathe, swathe, cave, gave, lave, nave, pave, rave, drave, grave, shave, stave, crave, ate, bate, fate, date, gate, hate, late, mate, pate, rate, sate, crate, prate, plate, state, skate, slate, waste, baste, haste, paste, chaste, taste, came, blame, dame, fame, frame, game, lame, flame, name, same, tame, frame, shame, cape, gape, nape, rape, grape, drape, crape, blaze, daze, gaze, haze, maze, raze, craze, graze, glaze, honorary, actuary, tributary, sedentary, primary, salutary, solitary, burglary, contrary, &c.

So for the sound of i long, as in marine, we have sometimes e, sometimes ee, sometimes ea, sometimes ie, as—

1st.—He, she, we, me, mete, glebe, theme, breve, veto, hero, zero, negro, ether, theist, deist, edict, fever, lever, metre, zenith, extreme, supreme, impede, serene, convene, gangrene, austere, cohere, adhere, revere, severe, interfere, persevere, secret, complete, concrete, secrete, obsolete, theorem, torpedo, inherent.

2d.—Fee, bee, lee, glee, flee, free, tree, see, three, eel, feel, keel, reel, peel, wheel, deem, seem, keen, green, queen, teens, ween, deed, feed, heed, meed, need, reed, seed, bleed, creed, leek, meek, sleek, seek, week, cheek, beef, reef, keep, sweep, weep, deep, peep, sleep, beech, speech, leech, spleen, compeer, between, beseech, discreet, steeple, vaneer, career, tureen, moreen, careen, redeem, agreed, settee, razee, degree, agree, decree, grandee, linseed, peevish, esteem, devotee, legatee, referee, repartee, patentee, absentee, privateer, muleteer, overseer, volunteer, chanticleer, domineer, gazetteer, genteel, indiscreet, steelyard, thirteen, &c.

3d.—Pea, tea, yea, flee, plea, bohea; each, beach, breach, bleach, teach, meach, peach; bleak, sneak, streak, speak, squeak, beak, peak, creak, teak, creak, freak, tweak, weak, bead, lead, read, plead, deaf, leaf, sheaf, beam, ream, dream, cream, stream, team, steam, seam, deal, heal, leal, meal, peal, seal, steal, veal, zeal, bean, dean, lean, mean, wean, yean; heap, cheap, leap, reap; ear, fear, hear, blear, clear, smear, near, spear, rear, drear, year, beard, east, beast, feast, least, yeast, eat, beat, feat, heat, meat, neat, peat, seat, wheat, bleat, cheat, treat, heath, sheathe, breathe, heave, weave, leave, treacle, eagle, eaglet, squeamish, dreary, weary, creature, impeach, anneal, appeal, reveal, endear, appear, arrear, besmear, defeat, release, increase, decrease, beneath, repeat, entreat, retreat, bereave, bequeath, cochineal, eatable, easterly, deanery.

4th. Where the e is silent; either, neither, seizure, surfeit, inveigle, forfeit, mullein, fief, chief, thief, brief, grief, field, shield, wield, yield, fiend, priest, belief, sieve, grieve, belief, achieve, retrieve, relieve, aggrieve, cashier, brigadier, grenadier, cannonier, cavalier, cordelier; also receive, conceive, perceive, deceive, deceit, conceit.

The sound of u is also written oe, o, ew, oo, and ou (silent o), shoe, canoe, woman, chew, brew, screw, threw, shrew, sew, dew, few, jew, mew, new, pew, coo, too, loo, woo, tattoo, bamboo, hindoo, food, good, hood, mood, rood, stood, wood, book, cook, hook, look, nook, rook, took, cool, drool, fool, stool, wool, spool, boom, broom, doom, bloom, groom, loom, gloom, room, boon, spoon, coon, swoon, loon, shalloon, moon, picaroon, noon, soon, poltroon, cocoon, platoon, festoon, monsoon, baboon, coop, droop, hoop, loop, poop, stoop, boor, moor, poor, goose, moose, noose, boot, coot, foot, hoot, loot, moot, root, soot, booty, roof, behoof, aloof, reproof, proof, groove, soothe, smooth, tooth, booth, boost, roost, pantaloon.

It is also written with a silent o, as in tour, croup, group, youth, wound, souvenir, surtout, cartouche, contour, amour, uncouth, accoutre, moustache, tambourine.

I have said that I give to my scholars "Mother Goose," as soon as they have mastered my first "Nursery Reading-Book." But this is for recreation; while all the important *work* is making the groups of exceptional words upon their slates, at my dictation. Sometimes these can be written on the blackboard, and copied into little books, by the children. When there are several ways of writing the same sound, I make several columns, and put at the head of each a word thus:—

i,	e,	ee,	ie,
pin,	me,	see,	grieve;

and then, mentioning different words, ask in which column they are to be put? The children are greatly interested in this exercise; and the effect of it is, to make them know the precise spelling of the words. When a column is finished, they are called on to read the words, and sometimes to repeat the group by heart.

I have not put all the words in the language in my groups; but enough for the purpose,—they can be filled up from the teacher's and children's memories.

The greater the anomaly, the more easily it is remembered, because the specimens are few, and the anomaly amuses.

Thus, I sometimes begin (after I have shown them how to write the extra vowels and consonants, and the diphthongs,) with the word *phthisic*; asking them all to write it on their slates as they think it should be; and then writing it myself, as it is, on the board. So I ask them to write *through*, which they will write *thru*. I then surprise them by writing it on the blackboard, and putting in the silent vowel and consonants. Then I ask them to write *bough*; and then *though*, and *dough*; then *trough*, which they will write troth; then laugh, draught, tough, which they will write with f for the gh. In reviewing the lesson the next day, all these words can be written in their manuscript books, with a lead-pencil. The book, which is the best one to follow Mother Goose, and perhaps might precede it, is Mrs. Mann's "Primer of Reading and Drawing." This begins with about twenty pages of words that can be read at once by those who have used the "First Nursery Reading-Book," because the Roman alphabet is a phonography for it all. Mrs. Mann's book is full of sentences that have beautiful meanings, and it contains some attractive stories. It has been out of print a long time; but a new edition is about being put to press.

But any book can be used by a person of judgment. The mother of the Wesleys always taught her children to read in the Bible from the beginning.

In good reading, words are not only to be pronounced, but to be read with expression; and this end is gained by its coming after object-learning. Unless a child conceives what a word means, he cannot have the appropriate emotion, and without the emotion he cannot read with expression. In hurrying children on to read faster than they can understand and feel, permanent bad habits are acquired, and especially the habit of reading without sufficiently filling the lungs with breath; and this not only makes disagreeable reading for the hearer; but is very injurious to the health of the reader.

Dr. H. F. Briggs, of New York, who teaches elocution as a means of health, proposes that there should be exercises of vocalizing,—uttering each vowel sound to express all kinds of emotion which the special vowel will express, and in all quantities and accents. Children are all naturally histrionic and will be amused in doing this. The vowel sounds educate emotions in those who utter them, and awaken them in those who hear. When pronounced with feeling, they come from the chest and abdomen and not from the head merely, and so give a general internal exercise that is healthy. Bronson's "Elocutionist" will give a teacher much assistance in this branch, though he has not worked out the thing so completely as Dr. Briggs has done.

It is proper to remark to those who measure the success of a school by the *rapidity* with which it teaches a child to read, that the thorough attainment of the art here proposed, requires *time*. But when attained, much is gained besides the mere reading,—namely, development of body, mind, and heart.

Besides, to those who are hereafter to be taught other languages it will be found of great advantage to have associated the vowel sounds of ark, ebb, ill, old, and rue, with the characters a, e, i, o, u, respectively. See for the proof of this, some articles on "Kraitsir's Significance of the Alphabet," published in "The North American Review" for 1849.

> The *First Nursery Reading Book* and Mrs. MANN's *Primer of Reading and Drawing* being out of print, Mr. E. STEIGER is about to print their substance together with the foregoing chapter as Preface to a *Primer of Reading and Writing, for the Intermediate Class.*

CHAPTER XII.

GRAMMAR AND LANGUAGES.

Mrs. Mann has suggested, in the last part of this volume, the first exercises in grammar. But grammar is the most abstract of sciences. There are at present few children sent to Kindergartens, who are not too young for the abstracting processes of classing words into parts of speech.

But it is a lesson of orthography, to lead the children to make the few changes which there are in English words, to denote grammatical modifications. For instance, let them write cat, and then say—"If you are talking about more than one cat, what do you say?" They will say *cats*. Let them write at the head of two columns—cat and cats. After some exercises on words adding s only, tell them to write box, and ask, "What if there are more than one?" Then go on and get groups of other irregularities, as changing f into ves, y into ies, &c. Having gone over the nouns, and told all their changes, for number, also letting the children write a list of the nouns that do not change for number, go into verbs, and give the few personal terminations thus: tell the children to write, *I cry*. Then say, "Would you say George cry?" "No," they will reply, "George *cries*." I say, "I have a book; but should I say, George have a book?" They will say,—"No; George has a book." Also by asking questions whose answers shall give the comparison of adjectives, these can be written; and finally the past tense and past participles of irregular verbs. In my own Kindergarten I have given to about half a dozen children who know how to read fluently, and can print very prettily, a little Latin. It is but a quarter of an hour's lesson, and is conducted in this wise:—Write down *am*. Now, that means love in Latin; but if you want to say he loves you, add *at*, which makes *amat*. Write down *ar*. That means plough; if you want to write *he ploughs* you write what? A bright child said *arat*. Now write down *cant*. That means sing. Now if you want to say he sings, you add what? *at*, then it is *cantat*. But if you want to say *to love* you must add *are* to *am*. They all said *amare*. Now, if you want to say to plough? *arare*; and to sing, *cantare*. Now make the whole sentence, he loves to sing. What is it he loves? They all wrote *amat cantare*. Now write he loves to plough. They wrote *amat arare*. I took the hint from Harkness's edition of "Arnold's First Lessons," and gave them six variations on the four regular conjugations, the infinitive and the third person singular of the present imperfect and future indicative, and Latinized their own names; and they were greatly entertained to improvise sentences, the most complicated of which was, O Helena, Anna loves to dance, Maria loves to sing. I give them no grammatical terms, but only English meanings, and shall not give any cases but the nominative and vocative at present; but I think I shall teach them to vary verbs throughout all the conjugations. It is perfectly easy to give so much of Latin grammar to children in the Kindergarten, because it will not involve the use of a book. They can have a manuscript book into which they can write their words and sentences, in print-letters.

French, so far as it can be taught by merely conversing with the children, is legitimate in the Kindergarten; also any other modern language. But let there be no books used, nor should French be written by the children, for it will confuse their English spelling, and not, like Latin words, aid it. In my Kindergarten, about a quarter of an hour a day is given to making French phrases by all but the smallest children. They have also been greatly interested in learning the French words of a play, which is a useful exercise in pronunciation. I will give the words here:—

L'Esturgeon (*Sturgeon*).
　　Commère Perche,
　　　Je vous salue!
　　Comment vous portez-vous?

La Perche (*Perch*).
　　Je me porte très bien, et vous?
　　　Quelle est l'heure pour le ragoût
　　Fait de sole et de morue?

La Sole et la Morue (*Sole and Cod*).
　　Commère Perche, je vous salue;
　　Nous autres ne serons pas un ragoût.

L'Esturgeon.
　　Commère Baleine,
　　Comment vous portez-vous?

La Baleine (*Whale*).
　　Très bien, et vous?

L'Esturgeon.
　　Pouvez-vous sauter en haut
　　　Comme moi,
　　Au dessus de l'eau?

La Baleine.
　　Je ne puis sauter si haut;
　　Mais je saurais faire jeter de l'eau.

L'Esturgeon.
　　Commère Hareng, je vous salue,
　　Dites moi, je prie, où allez-vous?

La Hareng (*Herring*).

Je vais chez moi, chercher les jeunes,
Alors nous irons à l'océan.

    L'Esturgeon.
Commère Brochet, je vous salue!
Commère Brochet, que mangez-vous?

Le Brochet (*Pike*).
  Je mange des truites
    Pour mon déjeuner,
  Et des éperlans
    Pour mon diner.

    L'Esturgeon.
Commère truite,
  Je vous salue!
Dites moi, je vous prie,
  Qu'avez-vous?

La Truite (*Trout*).
    Ah, par exemple,
      J'ai bien grand peur;
    Voilà le brocheton
    Même si de bonne heure!

    L'Esturgeon.
    Commère Requin,
      Je vous salue!
    Que faites-vous là
      Auprès du bateau.

Le Requin (*Shark*).
    Je veux manger
      Le petit garçon,
    Qui pêche dans l'eau.
      Pour l'éperlan.

L'Eperlan (*Smelt*).
Petit garçon,
Je vous salue!
Voilà la Requin
Près de moi, et près de vous.
(*Tous les poissons se plongent.*)

The play consists in each fish being represented by a child; and the little boy also. As the Sturgeon asks her questions, she jumps up and down, and as the fishes answer, they jump up and down, till all are in motion. But, before it is played, the whole must be learnt,—which is nearly a winter's work.

In the Kindergarten connected with Madame Kriege's Normal class in Boston, German is taught at the same time with English; or at least as soon as the children can read English with tolerable fluency.

And Mrs. Kriege would doubtless, if desired, teach the Normal scholars German; but to learn German they would need to remain in the training-school more than six months, the time she decides to be the least possible for preparation to be a Kindergartner.

CHAPTER XIII.

GEOGRAPHY.

Mr. Sheldon, in his "Elementary Instruction," has shown the way in which we may begin to teach geography without books. To proceed in that way, up to the point of drawing all maps, is feasible in a Kindergarten, if the children stay long enough. My children learn a great deal about the geographical locality of animals, from the natural history lessons given over the blocks. A "Picturesque Geography," compiled by Mrs. Mann, from the most brilliant descriptions of travellers, may by and by be printed, and it would be a good book to read to children. It should be read slowly, requiring them to tell what it makes them see in their fancy. This comprises a great deal of physical geography, and is a desirable precursor of political geography, which will be studied to most advantage by and by, with history. (But history is altogether beyond the Kindergarten.)

As soon as children know how to read, we advise that they be taught topography by Mr. Theodore Fay's atlas, according to his method,—which secures that they learn the maps by looking at the places as represented, and not by *words*, which can be learned without conveying the image, or an idea; and are easily forgotten.

CHAPTER XIV.

THE SECRET OF POWER.

In the foregoing pages I have done what I can, to make a Kindergarten Guide; not only for the use of those who undertake the new education, but in order to give parents a definite idea of the value of the new education to their children, and how they may aid rather than hinder its legitimate effect. Parents who live in places so isolated as to make a Kindergarten impossible, may also get some hints how to supply the want in some measure, by becoming themselves the playmates of their children.

I think it will be readily inferred, from what I have said, that the secret of power and success is *gradualism*. Any child can learn anything, if time and opportunity is given to go step by step. Then learning becomes as easy and agreeable as eating and drinking. Every degree of knowledge, also, must be practically used as soon as attained. It then becomes a power; makes the child a power in nature; and prepares him, when his spirit shall come into union with the God of Nature, and Father of Human Spirits, to become a power over Nature—"for the glory of God and relief of man's estate."

www.ingramcontent.com/pod-product-compliance
Lightning Source LLC
Chambersburg PA
CBHW081624100526
44590CB00021B/3583